Churchill's
Little
Redhead

For my children
Justin, Dominic, Alexander and Sophie
and my grandchildren
Archie, Max, Jesse and Rupert.

Churchill's Little Redhead

CELIA SANDYS

With an Introduction by
BARBARA TAYLOR BRADFORD

FONTHILL

www.fonthill.media
books@fonthill.media

First published in the United Kingdom
and the United States of America 2021

British Library Cataloguing in Publication Data:
A catalogue record for this book is available from the British Library

Copyright © Celia Sandys 2021

ISBN 978-1-78155-855-3

Typeset in 10.5pt on 13pt Sabon
Printed and bound in England

Contents

Acknowledgements

I would like to thank my publishers for believing that I had a story to tell, my friends and family and all those who were happy to share their memories and go with me on my journey down memory lane.

Special thanks to Barbara Taylor Bradford for her generous introduction also to Madeleine Kingsley and Stewart Binns who have both been a constant source of encouragement and advice.

My greatest gratitude goes to my grandfather who is, of course, the reason you are reading this.

Introduction

When Celia Sandys phoned me to ask if I would write the Introduction to her memoir, I said, 'Yes!' at once. Why wouldn't I? She is a dear friend; I knew she was a good writer, besides which she is the granddaughter of Sir Winston Churchill, my great hero.

In a funny sort of way, I grew up with Winston Churchill, although not quite the way she did.

In 1900, when Sir Winston was a young journalist, he was covering the Boer War. Arrested by the Boers, he managed to escape from jail. As he was leaving South Africa, he got up on the roof of the train he was on, waved his arms and shouted to no one but the countryside, 'Winston Bloody Churchill!'

In England, he was a hero, and when my grandmother, Esther Taylor, had her first child, a son, she called him Winston, after Churchill. So all through my childhood I heard the great man's name uttered time and again by my father's brothers and sisters. During the Second World War, when I was a small child, I heard the sonorous voice on the radio. Naturally, the entire Taylor family were Churchill fans and listened to all of his radio speeches. As did I.

Having assured Celia I would love to write the Introduction to her memoir, I waited with great anticipation for it to arrive. And because of its lovely, catchy title, I knew with certainty that she would have written about her grandfather. Obviously, she had grown up with him. As an avid devotee of his, I have read almost every book written about him. Now a memoir from Celia was coming, and when it arrived, I began to read it immediately.

I was captivated from the first page and could not put it down. To begin with, Celia is an extremely good writer and has written other books, always about her grandfather. She has a clear, precise style, and the words flow beautifully. She also has a clever turn of phrase, and she knows how to use words in a powerful way. Not surprising!

Her memoir starts with her childhood. Her mother was Diana Churchill, the oldest daughter of Clementine and Winston, and she was married to Duncan Sandys, a Tory politician and a minister in the British government.

Celia's childhood was lovely, and she was close to her older sister, Edwina, and brother, Julian. The Sandys family lived in London, but Celia writes much about going to stay with her grandparents at their country house, Chartwell Manor in Kent. Winston had bought the house in 1922, and it was his favorite place to live.

Celia's days at Chartwell were happy. She watched her grandfather painting, his hobby, and admired the finished paintings. She also watched him building walls, brick by brick, and creating waterfalls and ponds. Another pastime he enjoyed.

Because Celia was born in May 1943, she grew up in the war years. Consequently, her beloved grandpapa was not always readily available. Later, once the war years were over, she became Winston's travelling companion. But more of that later.

During the remaining years of the war, Celia and her siblings were surrounded by ruined buildings and rubble. Their mother was an air raid warden and a member of the St John's Ambulance Service. At that time, everyone was shaken by the loss of 43,000 in the Blitz of 1940–41. However, all believed in Winston, that he would save England.

Celia remembers that as a war baby she was dressed 'in the spirit of make do and mend'. She wore the baby clothes that her siblings had worn before her.

In the childhood part of her book, Celia points out that most people remember Winston, on 10 May 1940, standing on the steps of 10 Downing Street. He had just returned from Buckingham Palace. The king had made him the new prime minister. He had a cigar in his hand

and was making the V for Victory sign with the other. His hair was snow white and there was not much of it.

Celia explains that most people do not know that he was born with bright red hair. She, her brother, Julian, and sister, Edwina, have all inherited their grandpapa's red hair.

Celia's childhood fled by, and after going to Heathfield, a private girl's school, she found a job. Later on, in her twenties, she went to South Africa to visit her school friend, Mary Oppenheimer, and fell in love with South Africa. It was in Nairobi that she fell in love with a man as well. His name was Michael Kennedy, and he fell in love with her. Totally.

After a happy courtship, the two of them got married. Michael was a successful businessman and could easily support them and their son, Justin, when he was born. Celia also brought up Michael's daughter by his first wife. Her name was Nicky. The two became great friends, and they all lived together, enjoyed the good life.

Sadly, after five years, this marriage fell apart, and divorce proceedings were started. Celia returned to London and took their son, Justin, with her.

Thus began the years of life as a single mother, who had to work to support herself and her son. And work she did. She bought houses, remodelled them, and sold them for a profit. She sold art for a gallery, even though she admits she does not know much about art. Other jobs followed, many of which she calls mundane.

She also travelled the world, just as she had done as a young girl. For instance, when she was sixteen, Winston had taken her with him to stay with Aristotle Onassis at his villa in the south of France. Aristotle also invited them to cruise the Mediterranean and the Greek islands on his super yacht, the *Christina*, along with his wife, Tina.

It was on this four-week cruise that Celia saw great luxury at its best, or perhaps worst. Bathrooms had real gold taps, and the stools in the fancy bar had seats made of the foreskin of whales. Hearing that apparently brought gales of laughter from some of the guests.

One of them was Maria Callas, the great opera singer. Celia tells in her usual clear detail how she, and everyone else, watched Ari and Callas fall in love. Despite the presence of his wife. Their affair became public knowledge, and the world knew it was tumultuous and difficult. But it lasted for years.

Working, travelling when she could, and bringing up Justin occupied Celia and kept her busy. But then Celia met Dennis Walters, the Conservative MP for Westbury. He was recently divorced, and they soon became a couple. Dennis, like Michael, was an older man. However, this pleased Celia, and, of course, she was the ideal wife for a politician with her background. They were married in May 1970 at the British embassy in Paris, where Christopher Soames, her uncle, was the ambassador. There was a moment though when Celia wondered if she had made a mistake.

As it turned out, she had. Celia and Dennis separated in 1979. Their son, Dominic, was eight years old; Justin was twelve.

Once more, Celia Sandys was on her own, living on her wits, as she called it. She managed well, taking as her motto, KBO, used by her grandfather. It means 'Keep buggering on'. And that was what she did.

Celia's third marriage came some years later. Her new, and last, husband was Ken Perkins, a retired general of the British Army. Celia was forty-two years old; Ken was seventeen years older. But age had never mattered to her.

They married five weeks after they had moved into her apartment in Warwick Square. Her marriage to Ken was the one that lasted the longest. They were together for over twenty years and were extremely happy. After a miscarriage, Celia had a son, Alexander. And joy of joy to her, finally a daughter later, who they named Sophie.

I found this memoir gripping, very accessible, and intimate. I could not stop turning the pages. I was transported back to other eras and places, some of which I knew.

At times I laughed out loud, because Celia has a great sense of humor and can be very amusing on paper. I also learned a lot and was truly impressed by many things: Her enterprising nature, her endeavours, her willingness to work, her desire to love and be loved by the right man, and her genuine joy in her four children.

Her life has been quite extraordinary—adventurous, exciting, sorrowful on certain occasions, but quite often hilarious.

I was moved when she wrote of her mother's unexpected, and questionable, death and her sadness about it. There was more sorrow in store, when her beloved grandmother, Clementine, passed away at Chartwell.

Later in the book, when Celia described her grandpapa's last few days, I realized I had tears rolling down my cheeks.

After lingering for several days, the great Winston Churchill died on 24 January 1965 at his home in London. His entire family was with him in his bedroom, surrounding him with their love, and sadness, of course. Celia was kneeling close to him. She tells in the book how she heard several slight sighs and then one long sigh. And he was gone.

Sir Winston had always told his family he would die on the same day his father, Lord Randolph, had died. This seemed a rather strange claim. How could anyone predict the date of his own death? But Churchill had done just that. He passed away on the same date his father had.

When I closed the book, wishing there were more pages, I could not help thinking about Celia's grandpapa. I knew that if Winston Churchill were still alive and had read his granddaughter's memoir of her life, he would have been impressed and thrilled that she had inherited her talent with words from him. I am absolutely sure Winston would have flashed his smile, raised his hand to give her his V for Victory sign, knowing she had never given in.

Barbara Taylor Bradford

1

Tuesday's Child

According to the sixteenth-century rhyme, Tuesday's child is full of grace. My arrival on Tuesday, 18 May 1943, was neither smooth nor serene. My mother, Diana, the eldest daughter of Winston and Clementine Churchill, went into labour at her hairdresser in Bond Street. She usually enjoyed these breaks from her busy life as the wife of Duncan Sandys, the member of parliament for Norwood in South London and financial secretary to the War Office and mother of Julian, six, and Edwina, who was four

At the beginning of the war Diana had been one of the first women to enlist in the WRNS and later, after my father was invalided out of the army and my birth, she became a volunteer air raid warden and a member of the St John's Ambulance Service at a time when much of London was in ruins and shaken by the loss of 43,000 people in the Blitz of 1940–41. She would have relished a relaxed couple of hours reading glossy magazines under the dryer. Any such respite was, however, rudely interrupted by the unmistakeable signs that I was on the way, three weeks before I was due.

This was probably no great surprise as Edwina had been born eight weeks early and, as Nanny loved to tell us, had been drip-fed with a fountain pen. I have never understood how that worked but that was her story.

Diana was thirty-three years old and experienced enough in childbirth to know that I was arriving … and soon. Kathleen McCleod, her hairdresser who everyone called 'Miss Kathleen' loved telling me that I nearly appeared among the hairnets and the wash basins and threatened to do so again in the taxi that was summoned to speed us home to our flat in Westminster Gardens, just around the corner from the Houses of Parliament.

It was, quite literally, a hair-raising journey, as my mother made a hasty exit from the hairdressers with her wet hair wrapped in a towel. Perhaps this surprise delivery explains my taste for adventure and my life-long addiction for black cabs. Thankfully, Diana was soon safely at home in the reassuring care of our nanny, Miriam Buckles, a former hospital nurse. I was born at about six in the evening.

London was still a dangerous place to be. Although the endless days of bombing during The Blitz had gone, there were still air-raids and awful tragedies. At the beginning of 1943, the Luftwaffe had begun what were called 'Tip and Run' raids on London. In one of them, a 500 kg (1,100 lb) bomb was dropped in the middle of the day on Sandhurst Road School, Catford in south east London. It killed thirty-eight children and six staff and injured another sixty people. Many were buried for hours under the rubble.

Soon after that, at Bethnal Green tube station, which was being used as a shelter, the air-raid siren sounded at 8:17 p.m., producing a wave of people down the blacked-out staircase from the street. There was no panic, but three steps from the bottom, a middle-aged woman and a child fell over. Others fell around them until a mass of trapped bodies grew to nearly 300 helpless souls. A few managed to get free, but 173 people, most of them women and children, were crushed and asphyxiated.

That was the London I was born into. Of course, I have no memory of it. It was only as I grew up that the gravity of events surrounding my birth hit home and lent perspective to my thoughts. Entering the world in tough times has clearly done me no more harm than it has to Mick Jagger, or the *War Horse* writer Michael Morpurgo.

War babies were very much wanted babies, certainly by the government, as the birth rate had fallen below replacement level by 1939. Women were encouraged to recognise that babies were for the good of the nation and, as novelist Naomi Mitchison put it, 'one in the eye for Hitler.'

The Ministry of Food's campaign, 'Welcome Little Stranger' ensured that expectant mothers, known as 'Lord Woolton's preggies' and new-born babies received nine months of additional rations: orange juice, cod liver oil, vitamins A and D, an extra egg and an extra ration of meat. Lord Woolton's notorious wartime pie recipe may have been less than tasty, but his message to women was clear and strong: they too were soldiers in their own way, 'The army that guards the kitchen front in this war.'

As a war baby, I was dressed in the spirit of, *'make do and mend'*. I inherited the baby clothes that my older siblings had long outgrown; nothing was bought. Everything was either passed down or knitted by Nanny, a wardrobe that continued for most of my childhood.

Premature births seem to run in the family. My grandfather, Winston Churchill, a 'wonderfully pretty' boy, arrived seven weeks prematurely, after his mother, Jennie Jerome, fell while following the guns at a shoot at Blenheim Palace, the ancestral home of Churchill family home in Oxfordshire.

The intention had been for him to arrive with chloroform and a wet nurse, at the ready, in the London home of Jennie and her husband, the politician, Lord Randolph Churchill. As my great-grandmother laboured in a downstairs room at Blenheim, a letter from her mother-in-law, Frances, duchess of Marlborough, describes how they had, 'neither cradle nor baby linen nor anything ready.'

That, 'wonderfully pretty boy', of 1874, had become prime minister three years earlier, in the dark days of 1940. He was having dinner at The White House when he got the news that I had arrived and that he had a fourth grandchild. He and President Roosevelt drank a toast to my arrival, not a bad introduction to life for a little girl.

However, wetting the head of his new grandchild was of scant significance compared to the real business of my grandfather's visit to Washington. He was attending the third Washington Conference, codenamed, *Trident*, which was laying the plans for the invasion of Normandy, scheduled for the following year.

He spent the day of the 18th and much of the following night writing the speech he delivered to the US Congress the following day. It took him over nine hours to dictate it to his secretary, the wonderful Elizabeth Layton, who was portrayed so convincingly by Lily James in the 2017 film, *Darkest Hour.*

Grandpapa, as we called him, had a legendary way with words, and his Washington speech became one of his most memorable. It ended with the rousing words, 'By singleness of purpose, by steadfastness of conduct, by tenacity and endurance, such as we have so far displayed; by these means, and only these, can we discharge our duty to the future of the world and to the destiny of man.'

My arrival coincided with the turning of the tide of war. Three years earlier, Hitler's panzers were just twenty miles away across the Channel. At that time, Churchill was almost alone in his conviction that Britain could survive but he set about the seemingly impossible task of making the country believe him. In May of 1943, there was, at long last, good news.

The Soviet Red Army had held the German invasion on the Eastern Front and had brought victory at Stalingrad. The bitter fighting was draining Germany of vital resources and manpower. Erwin Rommel's Afrika Corps had been pushed out of North Africa and the amazing Dambuster raids on the Ruhr had been a success.

Perhaps most significantly, the Battle of the Atlantic had tipped in the Allies' favour. A combination of new radar technology, long-distance bombing raids and Bletchley Park's cracking of the secret Enigma codes for Germany's U-boats, put them at the Allies' mercy. 43 U-boats were sunk in a single month. The Germans called it, 'Black May'.

I spent those heady days in my nursery, oblivious to the significance of the critical events of the spring and summer of 1943. I was named Celia, but it was not my mother's first choice. She was going through a religious phase and wanted to call me Mary, but my grandmother, Clementine's youngest daughter was called Mary, and she did not want another Mary in the family. Angela was the next choice; perhaps I was particularly angelic! But my father did not like it; maybe he thought that I would not live up to its inferences. If he did, he was right!

So, I became Celia, Mary. I am not sure why. Celia is the Latin word for 'heavenly', which may have been a good compromise. My mother used to call me her 'bird of heaven' so perhaps that was the reason.

The whole family, including my grandfather, who was quite busy at the time, came to my christening at the church of St Barnabus in Pimlico.

When the vicar asked the godparents if they were churchgoers who would oversee my spiritual development, they all answered 'No'. So, he decided, there and then at the font, to add himself to the list of my supporters. I never saw him again but when I was confirmed he wrote to me, 'I will pray for you daily with my thirty-four other godchildren'. If he saw the others as little as he saw me, he would have been better off collecting stamps.

The last years of the war were not without incident in our part of London. At 3 a.m. on 1 July 1944, a V1 flying bomb slammed into the Peabody Building flats just off Westmoreland Terrace in Pimlico. Seven people were killed and eighty-five injured. Just four days later, a second V1 exploded on Westmoreland Terrace itself. Ten people were killed; sixty-two others were injured. Repair crews working on the earlier attack site were temporarily trapped in the rubble. Hundreds of people were made homeless; removal vans carried away the salvaged belongings of over 200 separate families.

These attacks were of particular significance for my father. He had been made minister of works in the government, and chairman of the War Cabinet Flying Bomb Counter-Measures Committee, with particular responsibility for dealing with the V-weapon threat. It put him at the helm of a long and difficult struggle as, in its death throes, Nazi Germany tried to use new rocket technology to grasp a victory from the jaws of defeat. With Germany on its knees, the ominous threat from the skies was finally overcome in March 1945, by which time over 10,000 weapons had been launched at Britain and almost 12,000 people had been killed.

It must have been a blessed relief to everyone but especially to my father. Over 20,000 houses a day were being damaged at the height of the campaign, leading to a critical housing shortage. The sound of the V1's engine was said to resemble, 'a motorbike misfiring'. When the rocket dived, and the propulsion unit cut out, there followed an eerie silence, bringing utter terror to those below. Such was the anxiety, by late August of 1944, a million-and-a-half people had left London and the output of commercial and industrial production was significantly undermined.

I may well have heard the impact of those 1944 explosions just a few hundred yards away but of course remained blissfully ignorant of their horror. Any talk of defeat was taboo in our house but that did not stop our nanny thinking and planning. Convinced, no doubt with good reason, that, if Hitler invaded Britain, his first targets would be the entire Churchill family, she was determined to be ready. There is no question that had any of us been in danger she would have given her life to save us without a moment's hesitation.

Most people picture Winston Churchill on 10 May 1940 standing on the steps of 10 Downing Street. having just returned from Buckingham Palace as the new prime minister, a cigar in one hand and making a V sign with the other; with snowy white hair and not much of it. What most people do not realise is that he was born with bright red hair.

My brother, Julian and sister, Edwina and I had all inherited our grandfather's red hair. I cannot give him all the credit or blame for this. Both our parents and two of our grandfathers had red hair so there was a strong chance that we would be called carrots, copper knob or ginger throughout our childhood. I certainly was.

Nanny knew she would have a problem trying to escape with three carrot-topped children, so she planned to dye our hair and take us to live with her parents in their pub in Liverpool. Fortunately, she did not have to put this plan into action but if she had, I am sure she would have succeeded, and we would probably have become good at pulling the pints. To this day, with a little help, my hair is still the vivid colour that prompted Grandpapa to call me the, 'Little Redhead'.

2

A Pink Cake

Like most people, my earliest memory is of something that was hugely important to me, but of little significance to anybody else. It was my third birthday a cake, a thing of wonder made by Madame Floris, the famous Soho baker who was Grandpapa's favourite. I can see it now, sugar pink, emblazoned with a cat. It was not as ornate or as large as the wonderfully elaborate birthday cakes she made for him, but, to me, it was magical. Pink is my favourite colour to this day.

By then the war was over, but we still had rationing and the country was on its knees financially. It was not the best of times for our family either. At the end of hostilities in Europe, VE Day was celebrated on 8 May 1945, just before my second birthday. As a result, the coalition government led by my grandfather had served its purpose and a general election was called for 5 July.

There had not been an election since 1935 and a broad political consensus had been critical to the stability of the coalition government. However, as soon as peace broke out, deep political differences emerged. Significantly, the desire for change from working-class voters had been growing since the harsh days of the 1930s and continued to fester even during the war. Popular opinion demanded that reforms be made in health, welfare, and education and that the power and influence of what was called the 'ruling class' needed reining in. This mood was reinforced by the privations of war, the loss of life and the economic hardships.

Despite Churchill's personal popularity, the election was an unforeseen landslide victory for Clement Attlee's Labour Party. It was regarded as a slap in the face for my grandfather, which indeed it was, considering the fact that he had held the country and the Allies together for five years.

Even so, perhaps he knew better than many that the result was much more about the changing face of Britain than a personal rejection of him. Although not a typical establishment figure, many of whom had deep reservations about him, he was nevertheless the grandson of a duke, a Conservative and an old-fashioned traditionalist.

Wherever he went while campaigning, he was greeted by rapturous crowds who cheered him to the echo. But they were praising their saviour, not the party he led. They adored him as their war leader, but not as their leader in peacetime. In the eyes of many, the post-war world needed to be about change and my grandfather embodied the past, a world that many preferred to condemn to history.

The Conservative Party lost 189 seats, including my father's South London constituency in Norwood. In 1935 he had got over 24,000 votes, almost 70 per cent. Ten years later, he got only 14,600, just over 41 per cent. Clement Attlee, who had served my grandfather loyally as deputy prime minister, was swept to power with a mandate to transform the country.

The moment came when Churchill realised that the election was lost. He was in his office with two people with whom he had shared so many wartime journeys and experiences, his secretary, Elizabeth Layton, and Patrick Kinna, his stenographer. Elizabeth told me that it was a very emotional experience. My grandfather was never ashamed of shedding a tear and she recalled, 'We all three had a good cry together.' Later, my grandmother told him, 'Winston, this may prove to be a blessing in disguise.' To which he replied, 'If so, it is very well disguised.'

Although profoundly hurt by the defeat, his own observations were insightful and say much about his generosity of spirit. To his doctor, Lord Moran, who talked about the 'ingratitude' of the British people, he replied, 'Oh no, they've had a very hard time.' Later, he said to Captain Richard Pim, who ran his famous wartime map room, 'They

are perfectly entitled to vote as they please. This is democracy. This is what we've been fighting for.'

In a remarkably perceptive letter to Lord Quickswood, who, had been his best man in 1908, Winston wrote:

> There was something pent-up in the British people after twenty years which required relief. My faith in the qualities of the British people remains unaltered. We must expect great changes which will be hard for the departing generation to adapt themselves to. The next two years will present difficulties of an unprecedented character, and it may well be that a Labour administration will have a much better chance of solving these than we.

Two days later, my mother and father were at Chequers, the very grand country residence of the prime minister in Buckinghamshire, with the rest of the family. They were with my grandparents for the last weekend there following the election defeat.

At dinner on Sunday, a Jeroboam of champagne, sent by Lord Melchett, was used for the toast. In his letter of thanks, the new leader of the opposition wrote, 'We drank the champagne with great delectation on what was my last night at Chequers.' The next day, when he signed the Chequers' visitors book, he wrote beneath his signature, 'Finis'. He was wrong of course. He would be prime minister again. That would be wonderful for him and exciting for me, as, when the time came, I would be able to remember Chequers and much else about being part of this famous family.

Perhaps the election defeat came as a relief to my parents. My mother had a young family and, relieved of her wartime duties, she could devote more time to us. For my father, the anxiety of standing up to the terror of Hitler's V-weapons had passed. But he also carried other burdens.

In April 1940, he served in the Norwegian Campaign with 51st Heavy Anti-Aircraft Regiment, Royal Artillery. On his return, he was being driven to his regiment in Wales by an army driver and a relief. My father, who was very tall, was in the back with his long legs sticking out between the front seats. The main driver had failed to wake his relief; there was a crash, in which both drivers were killed, and my father's legs were badly injured.

When my mother arrived at the hospital, the doctors gave her the unpleasant task of telling her husband that they needed to amputate both his legs below the knee. Realising how catastrophic that would be, he refused, suggesting that they remove the most damaged limb and patch-up the better one. In fact, they avoided making the choice and decided to put both legs in plaster to see how they healed. Amazingly, both feet survived, but he was left with a lifetime of pain. His ankles had to be fused, so he could 'rock', but not really walk. He had special shoes, which had thick, curved soles. These once prompted a woman to say 'Mr. Sandys, I do like your platform shoes.' She was mortified when she realised they were a medical necessity! I never knew my father when he could walk normally or run. At the sea he had to walk in backwards and fall back into the water. He was clearly in a lot of pain but never complained.

Although he may not have thought it at the time, perhaps losing his seat gave my father a chance to draw breath after the pressures of the war and come to terms with his injuries. For me, it meant that we became a more 'normal' family for a while; not that we were 'abnormal', but we were a product of our upbringing. It was not that my parents neglected us or did not care. Far from it. We knew they loved us and spent as much time with us as they could. But they were from a background that had nannies, cooks, and cleaners and, to them, our upbringing was normal, just like the one they had had.

My life at home revolved around three people: Nanny, Lukey and Gray-Gray. They were such an important part of our household that it really did not matter where our parents were, or what they were doing, because we had these three incredibly different women to care for us. They were paid about £4 a week, were fiercely loyal and devoted and gave me a wonderfully broad education about the real world; their world which was very different from ours.

Annie Gray came from Bermondsey. She started work at 4 a.m. every morning, cleaning offices on Millbank, before coming to us. She had no bath at home and used to go to the public baths once a week. When my parents told her, they were getting divorced she was so shocked that her hair fell out overnight. I have never forgotten seeing her the next day wearing a scarf to conceal the fact that all her hair had gone.

There was Hilda Lucas, Lukey, our cook, who called herself 'chief cook and bottle washer.' There was nothing fancy about her food, but she was a very good plain cook. Lukey had worked in some very grand houses and been married to a chauffeur who had died. During the war she had taken in evacuees at her home in Ilfracombe, but when they left, she came to work for us.

Ever-present in my life, she taught me to play gin rummy and whist and the realities of the second quarter of the twentieth century. Lukey had been in service, which gave me an extraordinary picture of what life was like beyond the confines of my upbringing. As a housemaid, she had lit the fires in the bedrooms at five in the morning. She also explained that life in the servants' hall could be as much fun as it was for the 'nobs' upstairs. She was a rather sad person and once told me that her husband had never seen her without her clothes on.

My mother must have been a very laid-back employer as every morning at eleven o'clock Lukey and Gray-Gray would down tools and walk down the road to the Duke of Wellington pub for their daily Guinness.

Nanny had been a hospital nurse, who came from The Wirral in Cheshire. She never went to the pub with Lukey and Gray-Gray as she had. 'taken the pledge' when she was young and did not drink. She did not have a 'scouse' accent but enough of a northern one for my mother to worry that we might imitate her Cheshire accent, complete with its flat vowels. I adored her and she became a major influence in my life. When I was little, I would lie on her bed every evening while she listened to 'The Archers' and would invariably fall asleep at the sound of the signature tune. Even now, so many years later, when I find myself humming it, it brings back happy memories of my darling nanny.

One of her favourite sayings was, 'Say that you can, and you will. It's all in the state of your mind.' She taught us to play the card game 'beggar my neighbour'. She used to read all the Georgette Heyer books and, when I was old enough and a new one came out, we used to share them, our favourite was, *These Old Shades*.

My happiest times were spent in the kitchen or staff sitting room, the fun place in the house, with these three women who called themselves the 'Three Musketeers', who taught me, 'The Lambeth Walk', 'Hands, Knees and Bumpsa-daisy' and 'Ten Green Bottles Sitting on a Wall'.

They were my family really, the people I grew up with. Lukey and Gray-Gray came with us to Chester Row after my parents' divorce and continued in my life until I left England eight years later. Much as I loved her, I would not have wanted her to look after my children. I would have been afraid that they would have loved her more than me. Nanny went to work for one of my mother's friends and then on to work for my sister Edwina, to look after her two boys. She stayed with Edwina until she died at the age of 80.

Like me, as a child, my grandfather had seen his nanny as the source of unconditional love and total loyalty. He wrote of her, 'My nurse was my confidante. Mrs Everest it was, who looked after me and tended all my wants. It was to her I poured out all my many troubles …' In turn, I knew that Nanny would die for me if she had to. And the day she actually did die was one of the saddest I have ever known. I cried every day for at least a month.

One day during the war, when London was being heavily bombed, and our parents were away, Nanny called Downing Street and was so forceful that an armoured car was sent to take us to safety at Chequers. Waiting on the steps was the prime minister, a title that meant nothing to me; to his grandchildren, he was simply, grandpapa. He greeted us with the words, 'Poor little shelter brats!' As a result of his relationship with Mrs Everest, my grandfather had a great affinity with my Nanny. I am sure she brought back happy memories of his old friend.

When my father lost his constituency in the 1945 general election, his mother and stepfather bought a dairy farm, Furze Down, near King's Somborne in Hampshire and asked him to run it for them. Granny had long been divorced from my grandfather, George Sandys, a former Life Guard, veteran of the British Expeditionary Force in the First World War and member of parliament for Wells. After their divorce, my grandmother, Mildred, who had been a Cameron before she married George Sandys, married Frederick Lister, who had also fought in the First World War, before retiring as a lieutenant colonel. He was a keen gardener and fiercely protective of what he, quite rightly, considered his domain. If he found us picking the strawberries or raspberries, he would appear to chase us away like Mr McGregor in pursuit of Peter Rabbit.

My parents were always very busy, especially my father, who, determined that Europe would never go to war again, threw himself into the foundation of the European movement. A belief in the importance of a more united Europe was widespread after the war and, with his father-in-law, my father was one of its leading supporters.

With my father as a prime mover, in May 1948, 800 delegates from Europe and observers from Canada and the United States gathered in The Hague in the Netherlands for the Congress of Europe. It was organised by the International Committee of the Movements for European Unity and presided over by my grandfather.

It is fascinating to think back to those early days of Europe and to imagine what my father and grandfather would make of the current situation and our relationship with our neighbours on the Continent.

3

A Tale of Three Childhoods

My childhood was lived in three very different settings and the contrast between them was extreme. My London life in Vincent Square in Westminster was by no means spartan, but, because of post-war rationing, there were no luxuries. We lived in a beautiful Georgian house overlooking the playing fields of Westminster School. I had one dress, my school uniform and three unattractive sweaters knitted by Nanny. One was royal blue; one was emerald green, and one was dark brown. Nanny was very good at most things, but she was not particularly good at knitting or with colours. Apart from pretty dresses that my mother brought back from her occasional visits to America, always identical ones for Edwina and me, and a smock dress for best, I had very drab clothes, but no one seemed to think it mattered what we children wore.

The fine underwear favoured by my mother was a different matter but became a distant memory because of the war. To save her clothing ration coupons she used to go to The White House, a beautiful and luxurious shop in New Bond Street, now long gone, to buy silk satin sheets, which were then cut up and made into french knickers.

My grandfather wrote of his mother she 'seemed to me like a fairy princess. She shone like the Evening Star. I loved her dearly but at a distance.' Two generations on, my own mother was not overly present, day-to-day. She was, on the whole, an unhappy person: she could be enchanting, but she had several nervous breakdowns and, consciously or unconsciously, we were always worried about her. She was however not at all distant but very demonstrative in her love for her children.

We were not encouraged to ask questions. I was twelve before I knew she had been married before, to John Bailey. One day I was in the garage with my father when I noticed a suitcase monogrammed with the initials DB and asked whose it was.

The answer came as quite a shock. My father explained that my mother had been married before to John Bailey, the son of a South African diamond magnate, Sir Abe Bailey who my grandfather had made friends with when he was a soldier in India. He had married my mother in December 1932, but it was not a happy union and they divorced in 1935. This is hardly surprising since my mother told me that she got married because she could not face the succession of huge meals at Chartwell and found that the man she married had a drink problem. Definitely out of the frying pan into the fire!

Many years later she took me to the Cooden Beach Hotel in Sussex and told me that was where she had informed her husband that the marriage was over and returned the considerable collection of jewellery, mainly diamonds, that he had given her. In every situation my mother behaved elegantly and correctly. I am not sure I would have been so ready to part with what must have been some lovely jewels.

My parents were married in September of that year. They met when Duncan was the Conservative candidate for Norwood and my uncle Randolph the independent candidate who was campaigning with his sister, Diana, as his main supporter. To Randolph's irritation Duncan walked off with a seat in parliament and his opponent's sister.

My mother's lifelong dread of getting fat led her to impose her own form of rationing: no white bread, cakes or biscuits were allowed at home. She did not want us to get fat either. But Nanny used to take Edwina and me for walks in St James's Park and treat us to her favourite madeira cake, which I still love. She never told us not to tell our mother but somehow, we knew to keep it to ourselves.

My father had memories of being teased at school because he called his mother 'mummy', so they were 'Mother' and 'Father 'to us. I never liked it, as, apart from it being a distant form of address, my friends all had mummies and daddies, so I felt different, a feeling which is never good in childhood.

Mother's rules were relaxed when we went out. It was a real occasion when we were taken to the Berkeley Hotel in Mayfair for lunch. There was no rationing in restaurants, so you could order whatever you wanted. She would have several cups of coffee and we would have as many ice creams as we could eat. Tea at Gunters on Curzon Street was also a special treat, but we would only go there if someone invited us. Sadly, the famous old place, renowned for its delicious ice cream, closed in the 1950s.

My grandfather recalled being, 'what grown-up people in their off-hand way called a 'troublesome boy'.' Edwina and I were never as badly behaved, but in the spring of 1953, we were taken to see the procession of the lying-in-state of Queen Mary and placed in a window by Big Ben. Our parents left us there while they went into Westminster Hall to wait for the cortège to arrive but gave us no instructions how to behave. We had a wonderful view, so did a photographer. The next morning there was a picture in the paper of our heads above the coffin roaring with laughter. We learned never to smile on a solemn occasion when there might be a camera around! Then of course, it was impossible to imagine a world where everyone would carry a phone and therefore have a camera in their pocket.

Holidays for my grandfather when he was a boy had included the contrasts of sailing on the royal yacht at Cowes or pleading with Nanny Everest to give him more money for the coconut shies on Skegness Beach. She refused, regarding these beach treats as wanton waste.

Our favourite holiday was running absolutely wild on Granny Sandys' Furze Down farm in Hampshire. We thought of it as our real home and it was where I spent most of my school holidays. There, we could do exactly what we wanted, and no one thought to stop us. It was not quite Gerald Durrell's *My Family and Other Animals* but pretty much its English equivalent. I would get up early and be down in the milking sheds when the cows were brought in to be milked and spend hours riding our ponies in the woods.

The farm manager's son, Alan, played doctors and patients with me. I was, of course, the patient and was expected to endure searching medical examinations. I always seemed to have something wrong with my appendix, or something down in that area! If my mother or nanny had known, they would have been horrified.

We had bicycles and ponies and were completely free in a way that does not exist now. I would fly down the hill on the main road completely out of control on my bike, not thinking a thing about it, whereas in London we would go no further than the sweet shop around the corner. I did like the Pony Club, but Granny was very competitive which removed some of the fun. One day Edwina and I were grooming our pony, Wendy, for a gymkhana when suddenly we realised that we had brushed away almost all of her tail! Needless to say, we were in bad trouble and not allowed to take part. My only moment of equestrian glory was when I came first in the leading rein class at Richmond Horse Show.

Furze Down had a tennis court which for some reason had a flagpole that flew the European Movement flag that my father had designed. It was a white E on a green background and was known as 'Dunc's trunks' or 'Sandys' pants'.

Granny and her husband, Freddy Lister, who, to differentiate him from our mother's father we called Grandaddy, lived in the grand part of the house, while we lived in the back wing, which was distinctly un-grand. Rationing continued for several years and I have vivid memories of tins of stewed beef and fruit. I can still picture pickled eggs in great pails and apples that had been stored for months. Although she was not the most domesticated person, my mother canned a lot of the fruit herself.

Life was pretty much without luxuries, but we did not starve. Everyone was very careful to avoid waste and we children were often told to eat all that we were given and not to forget 'the starving children in China'. I could not see the logic of this as it was clear that the food, I had left on my plate could never help those children. My mother, always figure conscious, had a different view, 'better in the waste than round the waist.'

Some Australian cousins used to send us boxes of crystallised fruits and lace handkerchiefs which seemed strangely impractical presents to send in wartime. Many of the treats and luxuries of my early life will always be associated with Chartwell, a magical part of my growing up. During the holidays if we were not in London or Furze Down, we would be there; frequently without our parents but always with Nanny.

In 1922, when Clementine was recovering from the birth of, Mary, her fifth child, my grandfather drove the older children nineteen miles into Kent to visit a house that was for sale. They ran around the house and the garden and he then asked if they liked it. They said they did and asked, 'can we have it?' He told them he had already bought it. The only problem was that he had not told his wife and she had not seen it. He clearly knew that if he had consulted her, she would have been unenthusiastic on the grounds of running expenses and the scope of the improvements that the financially irresponsible Winston would undoubtedly incur.

He bought Chartwell in 1922 and for forty years it became the centre of family life. Its purchase was the result of a bequest that he received from a distant cousin who died without direct heirs. All Clementine's worst fears were confirmed as Winston spent years creating waterfalls which tumbled down the hillside to a large lake and a heated swimming pool. She never had quite the same affection for it as her husband. He used to say, 'A day away from Chartwell is a day wasted'. Close to Westerham on the Weald of Kent, it is an imposing red-brick house with Tudor origins. He did not buy a house he bought a view and what a view he bought! The house has an outstandingly beautiful view over the Weald of Kent. Following the purchase, my grandfather wrote to the previous owner, saying, 'I am very glad indeed to have become the possessor of "Chartwell". I have been searching for two years for a home in the country and the site is the most beautiful and charming I have ever seen.'

There was another thing that might have influenced him. His beloved nanny, Mrs Everest, who came from Kent told him it was 'the garden of England and the best place in the world.' It was, in those days only about half an hour by car from the House of Commons which was an added bonus.

Life there could not have been more different from our house in Vincent Square. Clementine, with the help of experienced staff, provided a very comfortable and unstuffy home which family, friends and political colleagues loved to visit. It was the place her husband liked best and where he felt most relaxed.

Lady Diana Cooper, the wife of Alfred Duff Cooper, British ambassador in Paris, and a renowned society hostess and friend of

Clementine, found my grandfather to be 'a benevolent old codger, twinkling with humour, treated as a naughty child by his wife, and mercilessly teased by his daughters.' She recalled him:

> ... mobilising tired notables at a house party, to search for a lost poodle. Clemmie, sporting a green eyeshade on the tennis court would whack professional backhands. Guests were briefed to bone up beforehand on Bezique, Mah-jong or bridge as Churchill was sure to challenge them to one of his favourite games.

I only ever remember him playing Bezique.

After the war I believe that the only people in the world who took Winston Churchill for granted were his grandchildren. For us he was just our much-loved Grandpapa. As a child, I had no sense of my him being a great world figure. Only by seeing how people spoke about him and how they behaved when they were with him little by little it dawned on me that there was something very special about my mother's father with whom I spent a lot of time when I was growing up. In 1953 as we watched the Queen's coronation procession from a balcony on Whitehall we screamed with joy as Grandpapa leant right out of his carriage and waved to us with his hat. The excitement quite took my mind off the awful red, white, and blue bow that Nanny had made me wear in my hair.

My grandfather had an unerring sense for what children liked. He himself had loved his nursery toys, 'a real steam engine, a magic lantern and a collection of soldiers nearly a thousand strong.' One never-forgotten day, a present arrived with the message, 'Please look after him for me. Your loving Grandpapa.' In feverish excitement I unwrapped the odd-shaped parcel and found inside a life-size toy bulldog with a head that moved from side to side when It was pulled along on the wheels set into its paws. My mother explained that someone had sent it to grandpapa, and he thought that I might like it. I did, but I wanted to know why anyone would send him a toy dog when he had a real live one. Armed with the explanation that during the war he had been described as 'The Great British Bulldog', I set off to school determined to find out what sort of dogs my friends had for their grandfathers. I did not get any satisfactory answers.

At Chartwell, Edwina and I slept in a room above our grandfather's bedroom. Nanny was in charge of us, but we saw a good deal of our grandparents. We always went to say good morning as they had breakfast in their separate bedrooms. Surrounded by the newspapers, his cat snuggled up beside him, Rufus the poodle running around the room and Toby the budgerigar swooping in to share what titbits he could snatch we would find Grandpapa having his breakfast in bed.

Later, confident that he would appear, we waited patiently for him to be ready to go for a walk. Accompanied by Rufus, his brown poodle, we would set off to feed the fish which swam around in the ponds he had made himself. As he threw the food into the pond the fish would come to the surface to feed. With a puckish smile he would tell us, 'you see they know me'. We soon realised that they knew us just as well. We would then go down to the lake to see the black swans, a present from the Australian government. They were very fierce, and I never liked them.

Whenever I go back to Chartwell, which I love to do, I always go to visit what I assume are the descendants of the fish that I used to feed with Grandpapa. The last stop was the pigs. Grandpapa used to say, 'Dogs look up to us, cats look down on us, but pigs treat us as equals.' As he scratched their backs, the man who would win the Nobel Prize for literature could not think of anything more original to say to the pigs, than 'Oink, oink.'

My grandfather was not just a safe pair of hands for the nation. He built a large part of the walls for the kitchen garden and dreamed up ambitious improvements for the house and its 80-acre grounds. Not only chief planner, he was master of his own building works and to his delight was made a member of the bricklayers' union. Chartwell is built on the side of a hill and my grandfather, who had spent large parts of his school holidays at Blenheim where he had enjoyed the beautiful lake, was inspired to create a series of ponds and waterfalls going down to a swimming pool and a large lake in the valley below. The execution of this elaborate scheme more than lived up to my grandmother's fears of her husband's extravagance.

When he was at home, life revolved around his needs, and his routine. When we knew he was working we kept away but otherwise he was always pleased to see us. Children used to send him presents, one little boy sent a fish which became the basis for a permanent fish tank in the study, others sent teddy bears and pandas which he used as place-markers for any book he took out of the bookcases that lined the room.

We would go to say good morning to our grandmother, Clementine who would also be having her breakfast in bed. Never looking anything less than utterly beautiful, she would read the newspapers in white gloves to stop the newsprint blackening her fingers. She was a perfectionist. It was from her that I first grasped how important it was to make a house beautiful, but also comfortable and welcoming.

I got to know her much better after my mother died. These two important women in my early life had a loving but fragile relationship. Clementine was first and foremost her husband's wife. The four older children were brought up on the whole by nannies and governesses and it was only after the tragic death of their fourth child, Marigold, at the age of three, that things changed. Winston and Clementine's fifth child, Mary, was born the next year and a relation of Clementine's known in the family as Cousin Moppet came to look after her. Mary had a completely different and much more stable upbringing which was reflected in her character. My mother told me that she had left home and married for the first time for fear of getting fat. The conversation at meals was always very fascinating, and the people at the table always interesting, but for my mother there was just too much food. She said she could not stand another meal.

Perhaps my grandmother and mother were too alike, both a bit highly strung. Clementine at times needed a respite from the strains and stresses of everyday life. It was certainly never boring, but it must have been difficult living with Winston Churchill. Never knowing what was around the corner or what would happen politically. You can see from the letters between them that the minute he went away she would be off doing what she wanted, going to art galleries, and taking us to the theatre. When he was there, everything centred on him. She really needed her periods of rest and relaxation.

Quite often when we were expected at Chartwell, phone calls would be made asking if we had left yet. 'Is the little redhead coming?' my grandfather would ask his secretary. I never knew until many years later that that was what he called me. In those days, thanks to the scarcity of cars and the absence of traffic jams, it took only twenty-five minutes to drive from central London to Westerham.

We particularly enjoyed visiting the kitchens at Chartwell, where we would find my grandmother's wonderful cook dressed in a snowy white starched overall longing to give us some little treat. Georgina Landemare started her life as a scullery maid, but later married Paul Landemare, the famous French Chef at the Ritz Hotel, from whom she acquired her considerable skills. She produced very good food, which was a subtle blend of French style and basic British ingredients and traditional dishes; all very much to my grandfather's liking. He was not particularly concerned about food, but my grandmother was not just interested but also very knowledgeable and took endless trouble planning the menus.

An awful lot of eating took place at Chartwell, where you reeled from one meal to another. Lady Diana Cooper, immortalised Mrs Landemare as, 'Clemmie's famous cook' saying, 'she had to cater for moods of hunger or of fractious fatigue and cheerfully reorganise meals ordered for six at eight o-clock, into meals for twenty at 10:30 p.m.'

When I was young the country was still on rationing, but my grandparents had the farm at Chartwell to rely on for meat and dairy products. Not only that, they were always being given presents: caviar, foie gras, oysters and other delicacies. As soon as we children could hold a knife and fork and sit on a proper chair, we would be at the dining room regardless of the company.

Because he had had rather a bleak childhood himself my grandfather treasured his family life, and the atmosphere was always warm and loving. We would gather for the most elegant and sumptuous meals, every one of which was an occasion. Dressed as usual in his siren suits made of pin stripped flannel for day and of jewel coloured velvet with matching monogrammed slippers for the evenings, he was at his happiest surrounded by as many members of his family as possible. He had designed the siren suits himself during the war, when he knew that he would have to get out of bed in a hurry when the air-raid siren sounded, and the bombs started to drop.

I always loved going to Chartwell. When Nanny's back was turned, Edwina and I were as capable of mischief as any other young girls let loose to run wild in the country. One holiday, thinking of nothing better to do, we began playing with the taps near the goldfish pond. We turned them on and off with no obvious results, so, becoming bored, went away to find something more interesting to do. On our way back to the house we passed the pond and, to our horror, saw the fish splashing around in shallow puddles of water which were draining away before our eyes. We realised what had happened but had no idea how to reverse the damage to save them and avoid the unthinkable prospect of having to confess to killing Grandpapa's precious golden orfe. While we were debating what to do our uncle, Christopher Soames, arrived and became our saviour. He found the right tap and the water gushed into the pool just in time.

On one occasion, we managed to sink the rowing boat we had taken out on the lake and had to creep back into the house in very squelchy clothes. Nobody minded our pranks until the day we managed to break a whole croquet set. That particular piece of mayhem they did mind! I think my brother, Julian, had a lot to do with it, but my father made us all pay for a new set out of our pocket money, in proportion to our age. It took us years to pay off the debt.

However, our naughtiness was nothing compared to my grandfather's reported antics as a boy. He was flogged for stealing sugar from his school pantry and, by way of revenge, kicked the headmaster's straw hat to pieces.

Chartwell is now owned and managed by the National Trust, it has been restored and presented as it was when my grandparents lived there in the nineteen thirties. These were Churchill's 'wilderness years' when he was out of office and out of favour. Convinced that Germany was once more gearing up for war he was determined to be fully informed. Politicians came to tell him what was going on, or not going on, in the government and people came from Germany to update him on what Hitler was planning.

Chartwell is a veritable treasure house and visitors can still see, among other things, the beautiful Lalique crystal cockerel, symbol of the Free French, given to my grandmother by Charles de Gaulle and the hideous ceremonial silver, a gift from Josef Stalin after the Moscow Conference in 1944.

By far the greatest treasures, in my opinion, are his paintings. The house and studio have the largest collection and catalogue his travels between 1915 and 1960. He liked to go to places that were, 'batheable and paintable' and his paints always went with him wherever he travelled, even to the trenches in the First World War. He only painted one picture in the Second World War, in Marrakesh, after he had taken President Roosevelt there following the Casablanca Conference. The painting which he gave to the President was recently sold for more than eleven million dollars by Angelina Jolie. I wonder who got it when they split up?

Chartwell, although of course now different under National Trust ownership and open to the public, is still just as enchanting to me as it was all those years ago.

The rural homeliness and tranquillity of Furze Down and the relaxed luxury of Chartwell changed dramatically in the early 1950s. There had been a general election in 1950, which returned Clement Attlee's Labour government with a much-reduced majority of just five seats, a drastic reduction from the 146-seat landside of 1945.

Constituency boundary changes had worked against the Labour Party and perhaps the wholesale welfare state reforms introduced by Labour had proved to be too much for 'middle England'. In any case, my father was back in the House of Commons, winning Streatham, in south London, with a majority of over 10,000.

The shifting political landscape was not the only dramatic change in our lives. My father's mother died, and the Farm in Hampshire was sold. Our agrarian idyll had come to an end; we still had Chartwell but not for long.

Struggling with a small majority, Attlee went to the country again in October 1951, when, despite winning the popular vote, the Conservatives triumphed with a 17-seat majority. My father increased his vote in Streatham to over 27,000 and was soon appointed minister of supply in the new government. This was the beginning of a successful ministerial career.

Chartwell once more closed and we visited our grandparents at Chequers which, being the official country house of the prime minister was inevitably less relaxed.

The whole family would gather there for magical Christmases with a huge tree and beautifully wrapped presents set out in family groups around the great hall. My grandmother was a perfectionist in everything she did, and she certainly made Christmas very special.

In 1953 the family was thrown into a deep gloom. My grandfather had, during a dinner at Downing Street, suffered a severe stroke. I was only ten but was fully aware how worried everyone was as the house was filled with long faces and hushed whispers. He was taken to Chartwell and was for a while desperately ill but his 'never give in' attitude prevailed and three months later he proved he was better by making a successful speech at the Conservative Party conference. The country never knew how ill he had been as the proprietors of all the main newspapers, who were close friends, has ensured that the news never got out. This could never happen today.

After Grandpapa left office in 1955 Chartwell was opened once again and we spent a lot of time there. I was surprised to find that when someone counted all the entries in the visitors' book, one of the most precious and fascinating exhibits with so many famous names inscribed at key moments of our history, I had been one of the most frequent visitors, particularly in the later years.

I remember lovely, relaxed weekends playing croquet, eating delicious food, and watching my grandfather's favourite films after dinner. We would then go to bed with the next morning's newspapers which had been delivered while we were in the cinema. Like our grandparents we would always be brought our breakfast in bed.

Inevitably everyone wanted to meet Winston Churchill. My friends and acquaintances were no exception. I was cautious who I invited but never had any problem until one young man, who I liked a lot, told me he was going to be staying nearby. I invited him for Sunday lunch, he stayed for tea and when my grandmother asked if he would like to stay for dinner magically produced his dinner jacket from the car! He never called me again and I felt very let down and used by the experience. He was the last person I ever invited to Chartwell.

4

Schooled for a Belted Earl

Looking back, it is clear to me now that my education and my family's expectations were a poor preparation for adult life. I do not blame my parents for this. I was brought up in the same way as the daughters of their contemporaries. There was certainly no discussion of careers or of independence and very few girls I knew went to university. It was assumed that I would marry a belted earl or someone similar and continue a centuries-old tradition. At the very least, I would acquire a husband who would look after me financially and make my life secure and comfortable. In return, I would run his household and raise his children. This now seems to be a very narrow-minded attitude, but then, it was the way things were.

When I was three, I went to kindergarten at Lady Eden's School in Kensington, of which, my only memory is singing 'Oh what a beautiful morning' from the musical, *Oklahoma* which must have been on at the time. I then joined Edwina at the Francis Holland School near Sloane Square, a fashionable and conventional school. The uniform was typical of the post war period, horrid scratchy grey Harris tweed skirts, blue shirts, ties, and grey flannel blazers. We were awarded posture badges if we held our shoulders back and had an annual handwriting competition. The school terms, as the school magazine reported, 'went by easily and happily, marked by successes in work and games and some pleasant and interesting expeditions.'

The school was founded in 1878 by the Reverend Francis Holland and his wife, Mary, who was inspired by her reading of the life of Françoise d'Aubigné, the morganatic wife of France's King Louis XIV. She had come to the king's notice as governess to his illegitimate children. Then, as his wife, she had persuaded him to let her start a school, where she taught the children reading, literature, religion and music.

I am not sure quite how much high-minded French culture Mary Holland brought to the syllabus. One poetic offering for the school magazine ran:

> My brother is a naughty boy
> he turns his nanny grey;
> He spits his bread and butter out
> At teatime every day.

Nanny took me to school by bus and was meant to walk me back home. But we often ended up in the Moo Cow Milk Bar on Victoria Street. My Aunt Sarah and her glamorous husband, the society photographer Anthony Beauchamp, lived in a very beautiful house in Ebury Street, which backed on to the school playground. I would often lob my tennis ball over the wall into their garden. Then, with the excuse of collecting it, I would run round the corner where I knew I would get a warm welcome, a glass of orange juice and a chocolate biscuit. Anthony was working on a very popular television detective series, 'Fabian of the Yard'. One day when I was eleven or twelve, he asked if I would like to be in one of the episodes, I, of course was thrilled by the idea despite the fact that we didn't have a television and I had therefore practically never watched it. I could not wait to tell my mother whose immediate reaction was, 'Certainly not!'

There was one occasion when I had obviously behaved badly enough to be sent to be told off by Miss Bowden, the very elegant and formidable headmistress. I cannot remember the actual misdemeanour, but the moment is still very vivid. Miss Bowden having reprimanded me said she had considered but decided against withholding permission for me to attend my grandfather's birthday celebration in the Houses of Parliament. I remember thinking, 'she can't stop me going.' On 30 November 1954 Westminster Hall was the setting for the presentation of the Graham Sutherland portrait, the present from members of the House of Commons and the House of Lords.

The rumour was out that it was less than flattering and I heard my parents discussing what his reaction might be. He of course had the words which very politely indicated exactly what he thought of the grisly portrait in shades of yellow and grey with a hint that his fly buttons were not quite closed, 'This is a remarkable example of modern art.'

He was so upset by it that my grandmother promised that it would never be seen again. It never was. Grace Hamblin, who had worked in the family for many years, and her brother burned it at dead of night, so that it could never be exhibited in the future.

At school we played netball and lacrosse in the winter and rounders and tennis in the summer, I liked games as we called them, best of all and was in all the teams. We swam once a week at the Chelsea baths. The swimming coach was Mrs Cockburn a lovely lady who decided that I had potential and invited me to join the Mermaid Club and become one of her group of competitive swimmers which she coached at the Marshall Street baths off the Edgware Road. This meant endless hours of practice for me swimming lengths of the pool while poor Nanny sat and watched.

There were frequent swimming galas, from which, more often than not, I brought a trophy home. My parents were supportive from a distance, but I do not remember them ever coming to watch me swim in a race. My father however did occasionally come to the swimming baths to see me dive and bribed me to dive from higher and higher boards.

My mother at this time was suffering from depression and was in and out of hospital so could only watch my races on the odd occasion that the event I was swimming in was on television. My grandmother came on one occasion as she had been asked to present the prizes. Happily, I won my race and there was a photograph in the paper of a tubby little girl, in a black woollen bathing suit, receiving the silver cup from my very elegant grandmother.

Maybe I inherited the aquatic gene from my grandfather, who enjoyed the outdoor pool at Harrow, he wrote of it as follows:

The school possessed the biggest swimming-bath I had ever seen ... It was more like the bend of a river than a bath, and it had two bridges across it. Thither we used to repair for hours at a time, and bask between our dips, eating enormous buns, on the hot asphalt margin. The Harrow boys always swam naked, I wore my horrid woollen swimsuit.

My mother did not consider it an attractive sport and, afraid that I might want to pursue it, was relieved when I went to boarding school beyond the lure of the Mermaid Club. There I discovered to my dismay that while in the past, I had been able to win races, I was no match for the girls who had grown up in South Africa. It was small consolation that they were amazed that there was any competition in England for them.

I was twelve when I went to join Edwina at Heathfield School near Ascot. If I had stayed at the Francis Holland, I would have received a very good education in the company of, on the whole, seriously minded girls, many of whom went on to university. At that time ministers and members of parliament earned very little, so money was tight in our house and my grandfather paid the school fees.

The uniform for Heathfield came from Debenham and Freebody, a large department store in Wigmore Street. The long list of regulation items included a smart navy-blue coat with a velvet collar and a beautiful bright red cloak, which was the only optional item but cost the princely sum of £10. I remember having to make a big fuss before my mother agreed to let me have one. The daily uniform was a navy-blue skirt, a white shirt and green tie. There was a navy-blue pullover for every day and then, in the evening, we changed into our own skirts and sweaters. Most girls had unremarkable woollen cardigans, but a few had a drawerful of deliciously soft cashmere. Several drawers for the girl whose family owned one of the leading cashmere companies in Scotland.

My grandfather had been upset only to scrape into Harrow. He later reflected on exams, 'I should have liked to be asked to say what I knew. They always tried to ask what I did not know.' It was at Harrow, where despite numerous accidents and two floggings, young Winston first showed glimpses of the scholarly application that would mould his great career. In 1889, aged fourteen, he wrote an imaginary, but much praised, account of a battle between British and Russian forces in the

Crimea war that heralded his lifelong fascination with the military and the heroic. He also wrote a very good poem marking the epidemic of influenza that was sweeping through Europe. Both these literary efforts were considered worthy of being placed in the Harrow archives and therefore preserved for posterity. His schoolmasters would have been amazed if anyone had suggested that the unpromising schoolboy might go on to have a successful life let alone be voted, 'the Greatest Briton', a century later.

There was no problem getting into Heathfield, where I had a lovely time. But to say my years were academically undistinguished would not be an exaggeration. Ours was the kind of education you could have had at home from a governess before the war. Almost none of the 120 girls had serious thoughts about going to university and very few considered that one day they would have to do a job of work. The most successful girl of my generation at Heathfield was the famous and fashionable interior designer, Nina Campbell. One girl did tell the headmistress she was thinking about a degree and was told, 'Don't worry, you'll get over it.' One did get into Oxford and we were given a holiday.

The only careers talk we had was from a WRNS officer from the Royal Navy, who brought a very lovely navy-blue jacket to show us. She chose the prettiest girl in the school to model it but got no recruits. Unlike my grandfather, the military did not appeal to me or to any of the other girls.

Recently, I revisited Heathfield, curious to see how my alma mater has changed. In some ways, it was very similar: the same elegant white house overlooking the tennis courts, grass in my day, but now all-weather the portrait of the founder, Eleanor Wyatt, gazing down from her study wall; and the olde-worlde tuckshop, just as tempting now as it was then.

There is now much more academic success than in the fifties and sixties as is shown on the display board which lists the names of those who have graduated with first class honours in history, fashion, and neuroscience. The beautiful chapel, always the heart of the school, with its incense and polished pews, on which all leavers had their names carved, is exactly the same.

The girls still wear white dresses for special services, just as we did, but not the pretty net chapel caps, which, to keep them fresh, we kept in cigar boxes in our lockers. We never questioned where they got 120 cigar boxes but presumably the fathers were asked to provide them. They had clearly been there for ages so Edwina and I did not have to bring a Churchillian box which by now would have no doubt graduated from the pigeonholes in the hall to a glass cabinet! No one seemed to complain that we went to chapel two or three times a day. I loved the incense and still remember girls fainting during sung Eucharist on Sundays and dropping to the floor with a thump. We took turns in swinging the censor and used to compete to see how many we could make faint or walk out. After chapel, we had to run around the games fields in our school uniform.

Times have certainly moved on. Now, senior girls enjoy their workouts in a purpose-built fitness centre, where a sign reads, 'Sweating like a pig, Feeling like a fox'. I was quite envious of the modern facilities and the level of comfort that is way beyond anything a fifties' schoolgirl could have imagined. No more matron presiding over a room called *Hygeia*; no more aroma of smelly socks in the boot room and gone was the scent of stodgy suet in the dining room. Each year group has its own common room, with kettle and television, squashy sofas and in one, even a juicer!

Apparently, a lot of marmite and toast is eaten, despite more than ample school lunches and dinners, presented, as if in a hotel buffet, at an array of appetising food stations, with an enticing range of choices. You can pluck fresh fruit from a bowl and take your water, with or without slices of lemon. The girls come in for lunch as and when it suits them. We had to arrive at precise times in orderly lines and stand at our set places and wait for grace, *Benedictus Benedicat*.

The textile department now boasts banks of sewing machines; in my day there was only one. This was presided over by Miss Spray who happened to live in my father's constituency and therefore took a special interest in me. I would have loved the photography department with its own dark room and the chance to visit Florence and New York if you were into fine arts. The school motto, 'The merit of one is the honour of all' is a lot easier on the ear than 'Power Through Control', which is the engraved on the lily badge, the highest award for making a major contribution to school life. Despite the soft sounding name, it sounded like a despot's diktat or an advertisement for body-shaping corsets.

Altogether the school was far less luxurious then than it is now, I liked school so much that I preferred it to being at home. Home life in the late fifties was a rather sad time because my parents' marriage was in trouble and divorce was looming. They eventually divorced in 1956 when I was thirteen. I have no idea whether my mother's nervous breakdowns were the consequence of her less than happy marriage, or whether her neurosis ruined the marriage. Either way, I do not have any memories of my parents being happy.

I was quite a shy child. Edwina and I were both at Heathfield together for my first term and the girls would compete to see which one of us they could make blush first. There were times when I was not the most popular new girl because Edwina's presence gave me a false confidence that sometimes made me appear a bit cocky to her disapproving contemporaries especially when I didn't treat them with the respect they thought they deserved. This was understandable but difficult for me as they had been in and out of our house for several years and suddenly, I was meant to behave as though I barely knew them.

I settled down but mischief was never far away. One day, we decided to go sunbathing on the roof in our bras and pants. Someone had the bright idea to take some photographs, which we did. Just at that moment, a helicopter came over, so we all went and hid. The next day my father said he had come to visit me in his Ministry of Defence helicopter but could not find me. He might have seen more than he expected if we had not been alerted by the noise but of course I had no idea that it was him.

Not long after we were summoned to the headmistress's study. She had received a parcel of photographs we had sent to be developed at Boots the Chemist, which, with prudish wisdom, they had returned to her. She tore them up in front of us and threw them on the fire with great self-satisfaction. Gone were the days when she was always very nice to Edwina and me because she was having an affair with a friend of my mother's. Once he had dropped her, we felt the chill and no longer received the preferential treatment we had come to expect. She did not waste much time licking her wounds. Not long after she resigned as headmistress and married the chairman of the school governors.

I did not know much about romance. In fact, I was extremely naïve. There was a clear division between the girls who were innocent and those who were not, and you felt quite isolated if you were not included in the knowing whispering that went on.

When I was fifteen, I went to Eton for the 4th of June celebration. The day, which celebrates the birthday of George III, is when the boys, their boaters garlanded with flowers, have to stand up, oars pointing skywards, and, while it is moving, balance precariously in their eights' rowing boats. Most importantly, for the boys closeted in an all-male school, the 4th of June is a chance to invite a girl to join them for this glamorous occasion.

The boy who had invited me, sat me on his bed and kissed me. I was acutely embarrassed because I thought he might notice I was not wearing a bra, of which I had no need. Looking back, I now realise that this might have struck him as a bonus. Not only that, back at school, having no real grasp of the facts of life, I was very worried that, as a result of that kiss, I might be pregnant. Recently I had, after everyone else in my year, started my periods and they were not yet regular. This of course added to my concern, but I was too ashamed of my ignorance to ask anyone, particularly my more worldly friends. Eventually nature took its course, and I breathed a sigh of relief. We never did study human biology; the breeding habits of rabbits were as far as we got in the lessons given by the timid wife of the school chaplain.

The Etonian wrote me beautiful letters which I kept tied up with a red ribbon but after some weeks they suddenly stopped coming. I was so upset I threw them in the fire. A few days later I discovered he had been very ill and had gone away to recover. We remained good friends, but it seemed the romance had died with his illness. I wish I had kept the letters as they were really lovely.

The following year, during the summer holidays, when I was equally unsophisticated, my mother and I went on what used to be called a 'progression' around Ireland. She did it for me, to 'widen my horizons'. We went to some interesting places, including Castle Leslie in Monaghan, which belonged to cousins of my grandfather through his mother Lady Randolph Churchill, Jennie Jerome. Jennie's sister, Leonie married Sir John Leslie, a descendent of one of Ireland's oldest families, which claims descent from Attila the Hun. The castle is still in the family and is now a fashionable hotel and wedding venue where Paul McCartney married Heather Mills in 2002.

I was taken on a tour by Desmond Leslie, one of a long line of eccentric Leslies. A former spitfire pilot and a firm believer in flying saucers and alien visitations, he once punched the theatre critic, Bernard Levin, in front of a studio audience and eleven million viewers on live television. Levin had had been less than complimentary about, *Savagery and Delight,* a play starring Desmond's then wife, Agnes Bernelle. Levin was not a big man, but Desmond was. He was also very polite. He asked Levin to get up from his stool and explained what he was going to do and why, before delivering several blows that knocked Levin to the studio floor. Desmond was particularly keen to show me the room where his family used to hide and peep through the cupboard when couples came to spend their wedding night. He then Viennese-waltzed me around the ballroom and, in a gloomy underground passageway, tried to kiss me. I don't think this was the way my mother wanted, 'to widen my horizons'!

Despite being reasonably successful at school, I left without receiving the standard accolade in the form of a white bow, presented at the end of their schooldays to pupils who had shone. It mattered very much to me at the time, as I had been a prefect, head of house and captain of lacrosse as well as playing on all the school teams. I can only suppose it was withheld because I had left a term early and had not taken A-levels. Because hardly anyone stayed at school beyond their seventeenth birthday my year had been made to condense the two-year A-level courses into just one year. I knew I would not pass, so I saw no point in staying on and I persuaded my mother that it would be more useful for me to go to Paris and learn French.

Some years later, I was asked to give a speech at Heathfield on parent's day in which I decided to direct my remarks to the girls. As I was bluntly honest, it did not go down well with the headmistress. After diplomatically and truthfully observing how lucky they were to have so many wonderful opportunities and facilities I said that we never learned anything about the world of work and that we were really educated for marriage. At one point, the girls were stamping their feet and clapping their hands. The headmistress was not happy with the high-spirited response, 'Any more of that and we'll cancel the whole thing,' she bellowed furiously. There were also many prizes to be presented along with white bows to the girls who had made a particular contribution to the school which struck a chord with me.

As I handed them out, I remembered how upset I had been. Mine was the only speech that was not featured in the school magazine. The next week I went to the same event at Cheam, my youngest son's school, and realised what had been expected of me and that I had fallen a long way short of that expectation. The speaker was an educational expert who gave a very dry speech during which the children got more and more fidgety and the parents more and more sleepy.

I remained satisfied with my performance at Heathfield despite the headmistress's disapproval. Soon after I heard that she had been replaced.

I left Heathfield with the sort of education I might have received from a governess before the war, which put far too little emphasis on formal qualifications. The late fifties were a limbo time for women, somewhere between stay-at-home Mrs Miniver wives and confident working girls who wanted to be someone in their own right, not just someone's wife or mother. If I had been only a few years younger, the ethos would have been quite different. Everything changed in the sixties, when taking a degree was suddenly considered not just desirable but essential.

My parents did not encourage me to stay on at school. It amazes me now that I could just leave and head off to Paris. I was allowed to go because no one valued examinations; they did not matter. I was not a rebel, but it seemed I could do as I wished. If I had been my parents, I would have been going to talk to the headmistress all the time. There was nothing I did not know about my own children's education, or at least that I thought I knew! But no one was talking to Heathfield about my progress and 'work experience' had not been invented.

The Paris I was to experience was not meant to be fun or bohemian. I spent two terms at Mademoiselle Anita's finishing school. The first term was quite a shock and took me out of my comfort zone, having come from quite a cosy school environment. My mother and I had visited the school some months before and took the bus back to the airport. As we sat in the plane on walked my Grandfather's private secretary, Anthony Montague Brown. I said to my mother, 'Oh look! There's Anthony!' 'You haven't seen him,' she said. 'Don't recognise him. Don't say hello.' It was very puzzling, but she said it in such a way that, of course, I did as I was bid. Anthony was with someone who was not his wife. My mother was quite good at teaching us how to behave in tricky situations.

It was arranged that I would stay with a family in Paris, who proved to be very stuffy and very dull. They were impoverished French aristocracy who lived in a very grand flat in Neuilly, an elegant suburb but not in the centre of the city. The father was a marquis, the mother very shallow and formal, the daughter was horse-mad, and the son very handsome but not very clever. It was however very good for my image to be dropped at school on the back of his Vespa.

Fate threw this odd French family at me. If only I had gone to the marquis's much jollier sister and brother-in-law, who were meant to be my hosts, and their extremely nice and far more interesting children I would have had a much better time. But, impatient to get away, I decided to go a month earlier than planned. They were away and sent me temporarily to stay with their relations. The original arrangement would have been perfect. They were much more fun and lived right in the centre of Paris. I was far too shy to say that I did not want to stay in Neuilly, and they were determined not to lose the money they got paid to have me.

Appearances were very important to Madame, La Marquise. They had a Spanish couple looking after them. If the doorbell rang, the Spanish helper had to become 'the butler', stop whatever he was doing and put on his formal jacket to answer the door. It was all very prescribed and very ostentatious. The marquise was very stiff, and the marquis was always off somewhere with his mistress.

At Mlle Anita's we learned French in the morning and in the afternoon, we went to museums. The girls were all English-speaking, mostly from Britain or South Africa. I did not know any of them but made friends quickly. My French improved and became quite good until, years later, I started speaking Italian; then it deteriorated. But now, I can still hear the mistakes I make in French. In Italian, which I never learned formally, I do not hear my mistakes so am more relaxed.

Mlle Anita was famous for her classes called, 'Savoir-vivre' in which she warned that, 'if you let a man have your little finger, he'll take your whole body.' I do not remember hearing that warning myself, but, up to then, I had no need of it, whether it concerned a belted earl or one of the many young men I imagined myself in love with.

My parents' friend Rachel Ford, who had worked with my father and grandfather on the European Movement, rescued me from my somewhat dreary circumstances. She took me to the opera and the theatre and her flat became my home from home in Paris. We became devoted to each other, particularly after my mother's death, and remained so until she died thirty years later.

Every afternoon, at least fifteen of us would go to a gallery or a museum. At the end of the day, we would have an ice cream on the Champs Elysees and then I would tramp back to Neuilly. I think we suffered from an overexposure to culture and therefore did not benefit as much as we could have.

Mlle Anita's was not a finishing school in the sense of teaching you social graces. For that, you would have gone to Switzerland. Mlle Anita's was all about learning French.

During the holidays. I spent two wonderful weeks with the nice family in the Vendée, which was great fun, and then another two weeks with the stuffy lot in the South of France, which was far less fun. We went camping on the beach in the Camargue. We slept in tents on the beach. It was awful; the marquise, her daughter and I; all three of us in one tent, and her son in another. She was snobby, cold, and very formal. Finally, one day, fed up with the discomfort, I said I was going for a bath. I rented a room in a hotel and had the best and most expensive bath of my life. It cleaned out my holiday money but was unquestionably worth it. They thought I was completely mad. The whole experience was so horrible, it put me off camping until I went to Kenya when I was twenty and was then able to do it in great style and luxury.

My second term in Paris was much improved because I got to know some French girls, and some of my friends from Heathfield arrived. I cannot say I had a rip-roaring time in the city of love but was completely saved by Rachel. If she knew that I was going with friends to the cinema, she would be waiting outside because she was not going to let me go back to Neuilly on my own.

By then, she was working for Charlie Chaplin. Through her, I did meet him, but only when he was very old. He was delightful and beguilingly charming.

In December 1960 I left Paris, speaking pretty good French, neither beatnik nor black stocking, and certainly not finished. I had hardly got started.

5

Coming Out

In my youth, the phrase, 'coming out' meant something entirely different from what it does today. Back then, 'coming out' meant 'doing the season', a carousel of cocktail and tea parties in the early part of the year, followed by dances in grand London hotels or country houses; all designed to present 'eligible' young women as 'debutantes' into 'high society'.

By the time I became a deb, its historical purpose had run its course. It was begun in 1780 by George III to honour the birthday of his wife, Queen Charlotte. The daughters of the aristocracy, all dressed in white, would step up to curtsey to the birthday cake as a ritual entry into society. Despite the lack of royal involvement and the fact their debutantes were no longer presented at court the 'season' continued with a constant round of parties throughout the year.

The old tradition had ended in 1958, just three years before, when the young Queen Elizabeth put a stop to the formal presentations. At school some of the older girls, anxious not to miss out, took the days off to be presented in the last year. I did not mind that I was denied the opportunity especially when I remembered the unbecoming dress my sister Edwina had worn for her presentation. She was presented by my grandmother because my mother being divorced was not eligible to do it. In those days, in the aftermath of the abdication of King Edward

VIII a divorced person was not allowed at Court events or in the Royal Enclosure at Ascot. With the divorce of Princess Margaret all that changed.

1961 was a year that was typical of the sort of dramatic changes that marked the 'Swinging Sixties'. It was the year of the Cuban Missile Crisis, Yuri Gagarin becoming the first man to journey into space and the establishment of the United States' Peace Corps. It was also my 'deb' year, when tradition suggested that I spend the summer in search of a 'deb's delight', who would sweep me off my feet and deposit me on his country estate. Needless to say, I was far from ready to be 'swept' anywhere, but I did enjoy the frivolity of it all and the glamorous clothes.

I wore satin shoes from Lilley and Skinner carefully dyed to match my evening dresses from Belinda Bellville in Knightsbridge. Belinda had 'come out' herself and was very much the 'in' designer at the time. The list of people who have worn her clothes is impressive and includes: Princess Margaret, Audrey Hepburn, Jackie Kennedy, Elizabeth Taylor, Madonna, Jerry Hall, Helen Mirren, and Ivana Trump.

I had five or six ball gowns including a mandatory white one for Queen Charlotte's Ball, where the debutantes, all dressed in white, would curtsey to a huge cake that represented Queen Charlotte. The ball was meant to be the dazzling highlight of the entire season, but it was in fact, probably the most boring. The cake, an eccentrically huge, iced pyramid, is a tradition instigated by Queen Charlotte herself. Somewhat bizarrely, in the absence of the queen, it had by then become a symbol of the monarch to which the debutantes curtsied. I was greatly relieved that I did not have to curtsey to a cake!

When I woke up the morning after a dance my dress would be standing up in my bedroom supported by the voluminous stiff and sometimes hooped petticoats. Left to myself, I would have chosen my clothes from Mary Quant's Bazaar in the Kings Road or Annacat, beloved by everyone from Christine Keeler to the American ambassador's wife. It did not take me long to rebel but for the rest of that year I continued to dress in a ladylike way.

Around that time, Princess Margaret had said, with typically indiscreet bluntness, that the lord chamberlain's royal command to summon 1,400 girls a year for the presentations should end because the 'calibre' of young women was in decline. 'We had to put a stop to it. Every tart in London was getting in'. Times change, so perhaps a ceremony that came with the direction, 'if in possession, swords should be worn', was an outdated relic. Although some trappings of the debs' rituals survive, it is now not much more than a social novelty and charity balls have replaced the private dances.

I cannot claim to have been one of the 'Debs of the Year' in 1961. I was not fêted in *Jennifer's Diary*, a society column written by Betty Kenward; I was not selected to model at the Berkeley Dress Show; nor was I chosen to push the cake into the room at Queen Charlotte's Ball. I don't think that was anything to do with me but just that my mother, unlike a lot of the mothers, would have been totally unconcerned and certainly have made no effort to push me into the limelight. She just wanted me to have a good time and make some nice friends.

I had decided to have my dance in November, at the very end of the season, so that I would be able to invite my friends rather than a list of people I barely knew. We held it at *Quaglinos* in St James's. We had one of the most popular bands of the day and my uncle, Randolph, turned up at the dinner party beforehand with his station wagon full of flowers. This was a typically generous but impractical impulsive gesture. He had stripped his garden of everything in bloom and arrived just as we were about to sit down to dinner. I do not know how my mother dealt with it without causing huge offence and a major row. I wore a very beautiful, pale blue-green satin dress from Belinda Belleville. Sadly, there are no photographs of that night.

Quaglino's had become highly fashionable in the 1930s when the duke of Windsor and Evelyn Waugh regularly dined there, and the novelist Barbara Cartland found a real pearl in her oyster. It was there that the young Queen Elizabeth first ate out in a public restaurant, the first reigning monarch ever to do so.

I was concerned that, after so many parties, everyone would be bored by yet another dance. I need not have worried. From the moment my grandfather arrived it was a guaranteed success. He stayed until two in the morning tapping his feet to the music. Apart from his presence the only remarkable thing about my dance was that a new dance called the Twist was played that night for the first time at a debutante party.

The next night we were all exhausted, but my grandfather, displaying his inimitable stamina, went out for dinner again; at the Other Club, his own private dining club, founded in 1911 by him and his great friend, F. E. Smith, Lord Birkenhead.

Even with the demise of the royal rite of passage, many girls were really excited by the Season, which they saw marking their transition between being a schoolgirl and being an adult. It was something that I was expected to do, and I did not question it. All my friends from Heathfield were doing it. It was not a bad time; I met a few people and grew in confidence, but if I had been asked me whether I would like to do it again the following year, the answer would certainly have been 'no'.

In fact, partying for months on end was, I thought, fairly boring. It was not the most exciting of times for several other girls as well. I could not play at the time, but, had I been able to, I would have joined one of the distractions created by some of the girls, a bridge school that met in the loos of several of the grand hotels where many of the dances were held. After it was all over, and I was not swept off to his country pile by a deb's delight, the issue arose: what else to do with myself, apart from endless partying?

First, I was sent on a cookery course at Tante Marie School in Woking. The school was new and fashionable. It was established by the cookery writer, Iris Syrett, and named after Ann-Marie Taride. Tante Marie was her pseudonym when she wrote the French culinary bible of the 1920s, *La Veritable Cuisine de Famille*.

I only lasted five days in Woking. I did not see the point. We already had a perfectly good cook at home. I told my mother that if I stayed at Tante Marie's I was going to get fat, a prospect I knew would horrify her. She said, 'We can't have that, you'd better leave immediately.' So I did.

Then I went to do a secretarial course, which did not interest me at all. The school was called, somewhat quaintly, 'The Queens Secretarial College for Gentlewomen'. I knew that if you failed to attend every day in the first six weeks you would be thrown out, so I deliberately missed a day. They told my mother 'she seems to be so good at it, I think perhaps we should let her back.' Despite the concession, I said I was not going to return and that was that.

I then attempted a third accomplishment and went on a dressmaking course in Glebe Place, Chelsea. I made a few dresses that I actually wore and, were really rather nice. This was definitely worth doing and useful to this day. I do not make my own clothes but am quite capable of turning up a hem or doing a minor repair.

Despite being able to sew on a button it was clear that I had no marketable skills, leaving my father to conclude with some distress 'You'll never get a job anywhere.' So, I went for a job in Harrods, in the cheap, or relatively cheap, China Department. There was a very understanding man in charge called Mr Pinder. This was fortunate because, at the time, I was much occupied with my blossoming late-night social life.

One day he appeared with a party of visiting buyers to find me fast asleep on a pile of ramekin dishes. I waited for a severe reprimand but to my surprise He said, 'Miss Sandys, I think you should go home and have a little rest ... and have a good party tonight.' I was eighteen. I doubt a female boss would have been quite so indulgent.

My friends would ring up the department to talk to me and everyone knew that this was what interested me most. I earned £4 a week plus commission. There was one girl who would say, 'Miss Sandys. Telephone call for you!' It would always happen when I was about to make a really good sale, which she would then take over and claim the commission. When I realised what she was doing, I started doing it to her, which became quite amusing.

Looking back, the truth is, I was rather unsophisticated and quite shy. A major part of my inhibition was my relationships with boys. It seemed that they all knew who among the girls was totally innocent, and who was less so, with whom they could have more fun.

If you lived in the country, you could make friends at the pony club and grow up with boys who would become your friends. The girls who were relaxed in the company of boys were obviously more popular and had far more fun at dances. On the other hand, if you lived in London, as I did, you did not meet that many boys. My brother was much older and had long left home. I did not know any boys except the one I thought had got me pregnant with a kiss at Eton two years earlier and the son of one of my mother's great friends. He and I had been born a month apart and had the same monthly nurse to look after us and our mothers had decided light-heartedly that we should eventually marry one another.

There was one boy I liked whose father was one of my father's political colleagues. He invited me to a weekend house party at the family home of one of his friends. I thought it sounded fun, and my mother said I could go, but she wanted the address and phone number of the friend's mother with whom we would be staying. She then telephoned the house, only to be told by the butler that both the parents were on the *Queen Mary*, bound for America. So, it became all too clear what the boy's intentions were and that was that. It was embarrassing. I was never allowed to see him again. I cannot have been that keen because I do not remember feeling particularly upset. He was upset because his parents told him he could not have the car they had promised him.

I loved going to nightclubs like Mark Birley's newly opened Annabel's in Berkeley Square and the very romantic 400 Club in Leicester Square. Princess Margaret was always in the 400, which was known as the 'Night-time Headquarters of Society', where she would sit at a table called, 'The Royal Box'. The man, (in those days the girls never paid), had to buy the drinks by the bottle, which if not finished would be stored for his next visit. During the war it was a favourite place for a soldier's last night before returning to the front. As he ordered his bottle of whisky it is likely it crossed his mind that he might not live to finish it. There were unfortunately many bottles that were never reclaimed. Despite its popularity and romance the 400 was out of step with the 'swinging sixties' and little by little it was eclipsed by the sophistication and elegance of Annabel's and finally closed its doors for ever.

On one occasion, Prince William of Gloucester, who was a good friend of mine invited me to stay for the weekend at Barnwell Manor in Northamptonshire, the family home of his parents the duke and duchess of Gloucester. My mother bought me lots of new clothes to wear and impressed upon me that I must not put a foot wrong. My aunt Mary was delegated to teach me royal etiquette.

I couldn't understand the fuss until my mother explained that, at a dinner party during the war, my father, after praising the king, remarked that it was a pity that the duke of Gloucester spent so much time in Paris nightclubs. What my father did not realise was that the woman to whom he was talking was lady-in-waiting to Princess Alice, the duke's wife, and William's mother. So the story went straight back to her. My father was cold-shouldered by the Gloucesters for the rest of the war.

My visit did not get off to a perfect start. Determined to do the right thing I curtsied to the woman who came out of the house to greet me. She introduced herself as the lady-in- waiting, not the duchess herself!

It was not a relaxed weekend. Every time William's parents came into the room we were up and down curtsying and bowing and changing our clothes several times. As well as the 'suitable clothes' my mother had chosen for me I bought a very sexy green satin dress which made me feel good but probably shocked the duchess. William and I remained friends and he used to produce me from time to time to divert attention from what were considered 'less suitable girlfriends'. He sadly died when he crashed his plane a few years later. I had completed my 'coming out', but I was far from the finished article.

6

Travels with my Grandfather

Apart from a visit to Brittany when I was five, we never went abroad for a family holiday. My only memories are of being constantly sick. First on the plane and then as a result of a tummy bug which laid us all low and put us on a diet of boiled rice with a spoonful of jam, my first experience of French cuisine.

After the farm in Hampshire was sold my mother would take us to a rented house at the seaside. The first was on the beach at Angmering in Sussex, then to Frinton in Essex which we loved because life centred round the tennis club and we had a sense of freedom and independence. We would go to the beach in the afternoon to swim in the freezing sea and eat gritty sand-filled sandwiches, otherwise we spent our days playing in tennis tournaments.

My partner was a boy called William and he was a great example of how not to behave in a sporting endeavour. Whenever we lost a match, he would throw his racket on the ground usually breaking it. His doting mother would race off and buy him a new one. Even at ten I knew that was no way for a child to behave or for a parent to react. It was at Frinton that I went to the theatre for the first time. The play, by Agatha Christie, now called *And Then There Were None* had over the years to get rid of two politically incorrect titles. I could hardly watch as I found it so frightening. It gave me terribly nightmares and I refused to sleep without the light on for several months.

Edwina and I loved Frinton, but our parents decided they would prefer Bembridge in the Isle of Wight where they had friends and where the social activities were more sophisticated. We were enrolled in the Dinghy Club and tennis was replaced by sailing. Missing our tennis life, we never threw ourselves into sailing with quite the same enthusiasm. Over the next four years we managed to sink or lose two boats, but we did learn to sail.

I was ten when I was taken out of school for about three weeks to go with my mother to a clinic in Italy. She was recovering from a nervous breakdown and wanted me to accompany her. I was allowed the time off as long as I took work with me. We went with a very nice psychiatrist and his then slightly crazy girlfriend who became his wife. The doctors took me for rides on their Vespas, everyone was very kind, and I had a lovely time. My Aunt Sarah's parents-in-law Vivienne and Ernest Entwistle were also there. Their arrival a few days after ours was preceded by a telegram from Sarah and Anthony the flavour of which gave an indication of their way of life.

> We're having a drink on the patio,
> To send Ma and Pa to Alassio.
> We miss you a helluva lottio,
> If you were here, we'd be blottio.
> Love Sarah and Tonio.

After the war, everyone wanted to entertain my grandfather. Newspaper barons and financial tycoons threw open their houses. His favourite retreat was La Pausa, a house built for Coco Chanel by her lover, the duke of Westminster. Filled with fine art and furniture worthy of a museum, it was anything but stuffy. It had become the home of Emery Reves, my grandfather's foreign rights agent, and his young wife Wendy, who had been an American supermodel. They filled their home with luxury and laughter. The two men had known each other since before the war, when Emery, a Hungarian, had repeatedly published warnings about the threat of Nazi Germany which my grandfather helped him disseminate. He had been a regular visitor to Chartwell and an invaluable source of pre-war intelligence about Hitler's activities in Germany.

I first met Wendy when I was thirteen and went to dinner at La Pausa with my mother. I liked her at once and could see that her only desire was to make my grandfather happy. She had been horror-struck the first time he had been to her home. Emery gave her, a domestic perfectionist in a then unfinished house, only a few hours' notice of the honoured guest's arrival.

Before long, she had persuaded him to stay with them and to use their house as though it was his own. This he certainly did which pleased him and delighted his hosts. Wendy arranged a bedroom especially for his needs including a tray for his breakfast in bed specially carved to fit around his tummy. This is now a prized exhibit in the Churchill War Rooms. It was lovely to see him strolling around the garden in his large white Stetson hat that was a magnet for butterflies. My grandmother did not like the South of France or Wendy so, apart from a few brief visits, he went on his own and, taking Wendy's offer to use La Pausa as his own, invited family and friends to stay as well as Anthony Montague Brown, who frequently brought his wife Nonie, and another secretary.

The visits continued for about four years until one day Wendy invited Greek shipping magnate, Aristotle Onassis to dinner. Emery was horrified and told her it was a big mistake and that she would regret it. He was right. The evening was a huge failure. Onassis, anxious to impress Churchill managed to do exactly the opposite and went away upset by his gauche behaviour. He called Wendy the next day full of apologies and begged her to bring my grandfather for a drink on his yacht that evening. Curious to see the famous gin palace he agreed, and the evening passed off very well. Ari understandably was much more relaxed on his own turf and as they left, he invited his 'new friend' to go for a cruise on the *Christina*. Grandpapa accepted happy in the knowledge that this was something that Clementine would also enjoy.

A few weeks later the official invitation was sent informing them that apart from them Ari had invited the duke and duchess of Windsor and Emery and Wendy Reves. Thinking that he had asked the grandest couple that he knew together with the people who had introduced him to Winston he was naturally surprised and shocked to learn that the Windsors could not be invited because of possible offence to the queen after the abdication and that Clementine would not go if Wendy was there. They had to all be uninvited. This unenviable task fell to Anthony

Montague Browne. History does not relate how the duke and duchess reacted, but Wendy's response was unambiguous. The door of La Pausa was firmly shut and they never met again. Emery's prophecy came true.

Idle speculation has suggested that my grandmother was actually jealous, and that there was more than friendship between Wendy and Winston. There was no question of anything other than a very old man being charmed by a beautiful young woman for whom nothing was too much trouble if it added to his pleasure and contentment. It was in fact he who persuaded the twice-divorced Wendy that she and Emery should marry, even though they were perfectly happy just living together. He even stood as best man when they exchanged vows in the library at La Pausa. Certainly, he was beguiled by Wendy. But then, who would not have been by a beautiful thirty-five-year-old offering every comfort and anticipating every desire, whether it was caviar or having his friends and family to stay?

Everyone lost out. He continued to visit the South of France but for much shorter holidays at the Hotel de Paris in Monte Carlo. The rooftop suite was very nice but not quite the same as La Pausa. My grandmother lost her periods of respite, Grandpapa lost his ideal winter retreat and Wendy, and Emery lost their honoured guest.

Wendy had not known how to deal with my grandmother any more than my grandmother had known how to deal with her. Wendy was a creature of luxury and extravagance. My grandmother was more down to earth. I am sure she knew that my grandfather's lifelong attraction to other beautiful women was entirely platonic. He was not really a lady's man at all. Violet Bonham Carter, daughter of Prime Minister Henry Asquith, was a great friend for sixty years. She certainly loved him but although they remained friends for sixty years that love was unrequited. Throughout his life he always had one strong woman at his side, for the first twenty years it was his nanny, Mrs Everest, then his mother, Jennie. But Clementine was the love of his life. 'My most brilliant achievement' he later said, 'was my ability to persuade my wife to marry me.'

In January 1956, I went with my mother to the South of France. My uncle, Randolph Churchill invited us to join him for a drink aboard the *Christina*, where he was a guest of Aristotle Onassis. I was a shy twelve-year-old with no exposure to the high life and had never seen anything so extravagantly luxurious.

Onassis was one of the richest men in the world and he had bought the *Christina*, a decommissioned warship, for scrap in 1954. £4 million later and renamed for his wife, the opulent yacht set sail, an arcadia afloat on which some of the most legendary figures of the twentieth century were entertained and indulged. Princess Grace and Prince Rainier held their wedding reception on board. Actor Richard Burton observed to his host, 'I do not think there is a man or woman on earth who would not be seduced by the pure narcissism shamelessly flaunted on this boat.'

I was too young and unworldly to appreciate the marble bathrooms with gold fittings, or to be told that the bar stool seats were covered in whale foreskin. Later I heard how the normally reclusive Greta Garbo was sitting on one such stool when Onassis swaggered into the bar and said 'Madam, do you realise you are sitting on the biggest penis in the world?'

I was probably more impressed with the private seaplane on the top deck and the seawater swimming pool with a mosaic-tiled floor. When emptied, the pool floor could be raised to double up for dancing. Roderich Fick, the man Ari Onassis charged with refitting his ocean jewel had, 20 years earlier, also designed Hitler's Eagle's Nest at Berchtesgaden. Fick saw to it that every last nook, cranny, and onyx pillar had the Midas touch.

The decoration of the nine guest suites was inspired by the Greek islands after which they were named. Onassis's children, Alexander, and Christina, used to occupy the Chios suite and the Ithaca suite respectively, although Christina would give up her place when Greta Garbo, Maria Callas or Jackie Kennedy came aboard.

There were also the Santorini, Mykonos, Lesbos, Andros, Crete, Rhodes, and Corfu suites. All contained wood and stonework that had been brought in from the Greek islands, the beauty of the materials chosen to enhance the guests' pleasure.

The most beautiful suite was for Onassis himself. Located on the pilothouse deck, it consisted of three rooms: the stateroom, an office containing a Louis XV desk, and an ostentatious bathroom. In addition to gold fittings, the bathtub in blue marble was surrounded by a mosaic depicting aquatic scenes in the style of the lost palace of King Minos of Knossos.

In our supposedly sophisticated and politically correct modern world, his taste and demeanour might now be regarded as intolerably crude, but he was a man of his times; fabulously wealthy, unapologetic and unashamed of his virility. In Ari's Bar on the main deck, besides the foreskin stool seats, the footrests were whales' teeth, and the ivory armrests were engraved with scenes from *The Iliad* and *The Odyssey*, Onassis's favourite epics.

The crew included two chefs, one French and one Greek, a galley that offered the finest dishes and the rarest wines and a host who fussed over the smallest details of the menu. There were also two hairdressers, a butler, a Swedish masseuse, an elevator, and an operating theatre, complete with a radiography unit.

My grandfather was invited to cruise on the *Christina* several times between 1958 and 1963 and, in April 1959, I held my breath for her reply when he asked my mother if she and I would join him on a Mediterranean cruise. We were going to sail from Monte Carlo around the Greek Islands to Istanbul and back. I literally jumped for joy when she said yes, and I can still remember the pleasure on Grandpapa's face when he saw how delighted I was.

I was equally thrilled when my mother somehow persuaded my headmistress to give me a day off school to go clothes shopping for the journey. We bought a holiday wardrobe more suited to a trousseau than a teenage excursion on the Aegean. I was never so well equipped for any of my honeymoons. Racing round the shops, we gathered bathing suits, sundresses and what were then quaintly called 'play clothes': full skirts and sun tops, nautical shorts and sailor blouses. We bought my first high-heeled shoes, evening dresses and a string of emerald green beads, that my mother called 'costume jewellery'.

This was my first experience of travelling in 'Churchillian Style', an experience that probably spoiled me for all future foreign adventures, as it turned into so much more than a hedonistic school summer holiday.

None of us could have had any idea just how extraordinary those three and a half weeks would prove to be: a fateful, glamorous and dramatic voyage that saw the start of a legendary affair between our host, Ari and our fellow guest Maria Callas, 'La Divina', the revered American-born Greek soprano. It was a trip that transformed not only their lives, but those of Callas's ageing husband and manager, Battista Meneghini, and Tina Onassis, Ari's wife, whom we all found delightful and charming.

I was a fly on the wall as the scandal unfolded, two marriages fell apart and the tragedies that were to beset the Onassis family were set in motion. At the tender age of sixteen, I learned for the first time, outside romantic novels, about affairs of the heart. Travels with Grandpapa were a far better preparation for my colourful life ahead than school ever was.

We set off accompanied by a vast quantity of luggage and a huge entourage: my grandfather's private secretary, Anthony Montague Brown with his wife Nonie, his bodyguard, Edmund Murray, a police sergeant from Scotland Yard, his nurse, Roy Howells, who was officially his valet, and my grandmother's maid. Even Toby, my grandfather's budgerigar, was a passenger in the cavalcade of cars bound for Heathrow.

After a brief stop in the VIP lounge, we were chauffeured right to the steps of the aircraft. In those days you could smoke on the flight once the seat belt signs went off, but only cigarettes. In deference to my grandfather, the usual prohibition on cigars was waived all the way to Nice. There was no question of asking the great man to refrain from lighting up his ubiquitous Monte Cristo. In any case it is unlikely that he would have obeyed. During the war, when flying in unpressurised aircraft he was told he had to wear an oxygen mask. He agreed as long as it was adapted so that he could smoke his cigar.

At Nice, my grandfather was given, in all but name, a royal welcome, with red carpet and a fleet of motorcycles, sirens blazing, to escort his car along the Corniche to the Monaco border, where Monegasque outriders took over with the precision usually associated with the Brigade of Guards at Buckingham Palace. As soon as the harbour of Monte Carlo came into view, we could see the *Christina*, by far the most magnificent yacht in the harbour.

Ari and Tina were waiting at the gangway to greet us and usher aboard the Churchill travelling circus. Grandpapa immediately found his way to a large chair on the rear deck, where he puffed away contentedly at his cigar, Toby tweeting beside him in his cage. My grandparents had their own staterooms with a sitting room in between. My mother and I were shown to an unbelievably luxurious cabin on the starboard side. Maria Callas and her husband would be next door. As there was no question of unpacking for ourselves, there was an army of staff hovering to respond to our needs and desires, I went back on deck just in time to see Callas appearing at the bottom of the gangway.

Our family was not musical, and I had never been to the opera or, until a few days earlier, ever heard of Callas. I suspect that my grandfather was equally unfamiliar with this large, ungainly, seemingly slightly nervous woman now brought forward to meet him. Tall and very dark, Callas cut a striking, but to me slightly reptilian figure in heavily embroidered beige calico, with flat sandals on her sizeable feet. By contrast, Tina Onassis, was blonde and petite, enchanting in her tiny-waisted summer dress and high heeled sandals.

A local reporter, who can only have been watching from a distance and way out of earshot, gave his own, neatly fabricated version of this first encounter between the elder statesman and the celebrated soprano. He said that Churchill took her hand without getting to his feet as Callas bowed. Toby the budgerigar then broke the ice and raised a laugh by saying one word, 'Kiss'. This was pure invention as the bird had only one phrase in his repertoire, 'My name is Toby'.

That night we dined under the stars on the terrace of the Hotel de Paris. The Mediterranean sparkled under the night sky as we guests got to know each other and subtly sized each other up. My grandfather was clearly entranced by Tina, a true fairy princess.

Callas appeared transformed, a model of magnificence in her heavily beaded, black lace evening dress. That night she lived up to her reputation as the most illustrious diva in the world. You could not miss the fact that Ari was powerfully charismatic, but I do not think anyone recognised Callas' extreme vulnerability at the time. We thought she was a troublesome prima donna. Certainly, none of us foresaw that the stage was being set for a tempestuous love story that would fascinate the world for years. Ari had already met Maria before in the spring, when she had sung for the first time at the Paris Opera. That evening, it seemed only natural for him to sit beside her as the ever-attentive host.

I was already having fun and was extremely excited at the prospect of the adventures ahead. As we sailed into Portofino harbour the next morning I was enchanted by the coloured houses, clustered hugger mugger against the hillsides, which they splashed with shades of pink, yellow, terracotta and green. Toby was flying round Grandpapa's cabin when I went to tell him of the scene, a view that I was sure would appeal to his painter's eye.

My grandparents stayed on deck, waving off the women, as we set off for a tour around the town. Tina was once again beautifully turned out. Even though I felt I passed muster, I took one look at her understated chic and realised that she was perfectly dressed. By contrast Callas by day seemed to get it entirely wrong. She wore a garishly coloured floral jumpsuit that could have been run up from chintz curtains and became increasingly awkward and irritable as we were followed everywhere by paparazzi.

That evening, it was my turn to feel ill at ease as Onassis swept us off to his favourite, shadowy and smoky nightclub. Bored and wondering why people liked night clubs so much, I had never been to one before, I was looking forward to leaving when a tall young man approached our table and asked me to dance. I was about to refuse when I felt my mother's firm hand in the small of my back, propelling me to my feet. I had never been a rebel, but I did wonder why she was so pressing. She had good reason. She was not about to let me miss my first dance in a nightclub with the future King Juan Carlos of Spain.

As we circled the dance floor, I tried to make conversation. After a short while he said, 'You don't recognise me, do you?' Realising from my expression that I had not a clue who he was he told me that he had met me when he had accompanied his father to pay their respects to my grandfather that morning. This was clearly a case of 'all kings looking alike in the dark'! Sixteen years later when the monarchy was restored on the death of General Franco, he became the King of Spain.

When we reached the Island of Capri in the Bay of Naples, we witnessed a musical stand-off between our resident diva and the music hall singer and actress Gracie Fields who came on board for the evening. There could not have been a greater contrast between the precious star of opera and the lass from Lancashire, who, when it was once suggested that she try grand opera declined, saying, 'I know where I belong.'

'Our Gracie' was soon serenading my grandfather with the latest hit, 'Volare', and then gathered us all around the piano singing old wartime songs. Clearly unimpressed, Callas could only fake jollity as she sang along to 'Daisy Daisy give me your answer do.' Nothing was quite what it seemed. I was mourning the tear in my brand-new silk Emilio Pucci trousers and my grandfather, despite the fact that music hall was far more to his taste than opera, whispered to Anthony, 'God's teeth! How long is this going on for!'

King Canute was famously unable to hold back the tide, but the very next night Onassis almost made us believe he could control nature as completely as he commanded great wealth. He called us all on deck to see Stromboli, the smoking volcano which looms over Capri. Fancying more fireworks for his guests, he pressed the boat's siren and called upon the volcano to put on a show. As if on cue, Stromboli erupted, with a flow of glowing red lava. We were duly amazed, but for Ari it was a case of, 'beware of what you wish for.' He was visibly shaken by what he felt, only too justifiably as events unfolded, was a bad omen.

Ari had Callas in his seductive sights, but to us she was like a swarm of jellyfish in our turquoise sea. Amidst all this lavish luxury she always found something to complain about. If the air conditioning was on, she wanted it off, if it was off, she wanted it on. If the stabilisers were up, she wanted them down and if they were down, she wanted them up. It was as though she was making a fuss to make her presence felt. In this she certainly succeeded and particularly aggravated us by trying to feed my grandfather ice cream from her spoon. He did not pay much attention but that was the moment when our patience ran out. By contrast, Tina's light flirtation with her most honoured guest rather charmed all three generations of his women, wife, daughter and granddaughter, and made us smile.

Just after we had passed Athens to moor in the bay beneath the Temple of Poseidon at Cape Sounion, the Greek prime minister and British ambassador and their wives came on board for dinner. A rather stilted evening could have deteriorated even more when my mother, intending to lift the rather tense atmosphere, decided to try something that Ari had shown us the night before. He was very proud of his new wine glasses which were so thin you could bend them, and he enjoyed demonstrating their flexibility. She picked up her exquisite Baccarat glass and raised it saying, 'Look Ambassador these glasses bend.'

Lacking her host's much rehearsed dexterity she squeezed too hard and a shower of Chateau Lafitte cascaded down his pristine white dinner jacket. The horrified silence was only broken when she said, 'I wish I had chosen the white wine glass.' Instead, the mood lightened and even more so when, after the ambassadorial jacket had been whisked away to be cleaned, Clementine draped her fur wrap around his shoulders and Grandpapa, ever emotional, recited from his still whip-sharp memory, a quatrain from Lord Byron. The mad, bad, and dangerous poet had carved his name on a pillar of the temple above us.

The verse my grandfather chose happened to be from *Don Juan*. It was so apt, you could not miss the sense of something stirring between Ari, himself a notorious Don Juan, and Callas. Even his children, Christina, and Alexander young though they were must have sensed the chemistry.

Grandmama, my mother and I would meet every night in Clementine's cabin, to gossip about what we had seen. We had disliked Callas well before this turn of events and felt increasingly sorry for Tina, who took so much care that we should be happy and have a lovely time. We were very much on her side, so we found it wickedly satisfying when we visited the glorious Ancient Greek amphitheatre of Epidaurus. There was a magnificent display of flowers prepared by the local people in the shape of a 'V'.

Callas, partly because of her Greek ancestry and partly because she could not for one second imagine herself playing second fiddle to anyone and certainly had no idea that the display referred to my grandfather's famous V sign, turned to my mother and exclaimed, 'What beautiful flowers! What kind people. But tell me, Diana, why are they in the shape of a V?' 'Because, Maria, they are not for you.' my mother replied, 'they are for Papa.' The venomous look on Callas' face spoke volumes. I did feel sorry for her as she had sung there on several occasions.

By the time we reached the stunningly evocative island of Santorini in the Cyclades, Maria had her own victory. When we came down for dinner one night, two of the party were missing and Tina told us that Ari and Callas had already eaten. They were apparently having a Chinese dinner in another part of the yacht. We struggled through dinner and the evening became a lesson in managing a social disaster. It seemed like another ill omen when, on our last evening on Rhodes, Ari misjudged a dive and struck his head on the bottom of the pool. He was briefly unconscious but pronounced recovered by his doctor and brother-in-law Theodore Garoufaldis, who, with Anthony Montague Brown, had helped pull him out of the water. Anthony always said that this blow to his head permanently affected Ari's personality.

Visiting the Valley of the Butterflies on Rhodes was extraordinary. It was like seeing the world through a giant kaleidoscope in which shades of red and gold intertwined as millions of tiger moths fluttered around, illuminated by sunlight glinting through the trees. I knew that my grandfather had aged over recent years, but he seemed rejuvenated as one superb sight followed another on our journey. Although by no means oblivious to the Greek drama playing out in front of him, he seemed very content on the yacht, and we enjoyed seeing his happiness as we sailed from one glorious place to another.

I flew home that August much worldlier than when I had left and feeling that I had become much closer to my grandparents in those four weeks we spent together at close quarters on the *Christina*.

It was Callas' heart, however, that would be permanently broken by their love affair. Even at the height of her fame she was insecure and, having had a platonic marriage for some years, believed Onassis to be her destiny. 'I cannot fight it; its force is beyond us', she finally confessed to her husband.

She remained slavishly and totally in love with this modern Ulysses, a man more than 25 years her senior, but he was soon distracted. Their relationship became increasingly on-off and famously tempestuous. He tried to win back Tina and when that failed began an affair with Lee Radziwill, the sister of Jackie Kennedy. Maria was devastated when he cast her off for Jackie; she had only ever been his mistress. Jackie was to be his wife. 'First I lost my voice, then I lost my figure and then I lost Onassis', she lamented. A sad and increasingly isolated figure, Callas died in Paris in 1977, at the age of fifty-three. Onassis married Jackie Kennedy in 1968. After the death of his son, Alexander in a plane crash in 1973, his health deteriorated, and he died of respiratory failure in 1975 at the age of sixty-nine.

The Mediterranean still evokes for me so many memories of my grandfather with whom I visited the South of France several times following that incredible cruise on the *Christina*.

My brother, Julian and sister, Edwina and cousin, Winston were already embarking on the early steps of their adult lives and my other cousins were still at school. I was lucky enough to be an available grandchild of an appropriate age to accompany him on peaceful, painting holidays in the warmth of the Mediterranean sun. We would stay in the Hotel de a Paris in Monte Carlo and sit together on the balcony looking down at the yachts in the harbour, go for drives and picnics but he was always at his happiest seated at his easel with a paintbrush in his hand. All of these activities were very nice but for me the very best thing of all was that, just for a few days, I had to myself the grandfather the whole world thought they owned. In 1960 the day came when he had to give up painting. Sometimes I dream that he is fulfilling his desire for the afterlife. Thirty years before he had written, 'When I get to heaven, I mean to spend a considerable portion of my first million years in painting and get to the bottom of the subject.' I hope he is up there on his cloud painting away.

On one occasion an American submarine was docked in Nice and they invited Grandpapa to visit. I think there was something special about it. Possibly it was a nuclear submarine but as I had never been on a submarine I was thrilled when he asked me to go in his place. They must have been very disappointed with this poor substitute when I turned up with Anthony Montague Browne, but they didn't show it. I was not particularly interested in the technicalities but was very happy to be shown the ice cream making machine!

From the day he received his first pocket money at the age of seven Winston's expenses always exceeded his income. He was as a result very understanding about money. He would often ask me 'Are you all right for money?' Never waiting for a reply, he would take a wad of notes out of the drawer in his bedside table and thrust them into my hand. I always imagined that this was a result of a late-night visit to the casino which he could get to via a secret underground passage which ran from the hotel lobby, under the square and rose up in the casino without anyone knowing that he had gone. My grandmother hated him gambling, but I certainly appreciated the proceeds!

Perhaps the most memorable event of the times I was with him took place in the summer of 1962. I was staying with him and his private secretary, Anthony Montague Brown as usual at the Hotel de Paris when he fell and broke his hip a serious accident for a man in his eighty-eighth year. As Anthony and I walked to the hospital he said, 'I am afraid that he is not going to make it.' This was not what I wanted to hear.

When we arrived in his hospital room, he was lying in bed looking incredibly frail surrounded by what seemed like an army of doctors and nurses. Clearly, they had all been determined to see their famous patient. He asked them all to leave and immediately turned to Anthony saying, 'I want to die in England. You'll make that happen.' When he did not get an immediate answer he said, 'Promise me Anthony.' 'I promise', said Anthony.

As we walked back to the hotel in sombre mood Anthony said, 'I am afraid that is a promise I will not be able to keep.' However, he immediately called 10 Downing Street and after a conversation with the prime minister, Harold MacMillan, told me that an RAF ambulance plane was coming to take us back to London in the morning.

Lying on a stretcher bed which was placed on the lift that took the food onto the plane he was wheeled into the stripped down body of the aircraft and a chair was brought for me to sit beside him. He looked terribly ill and, with Anthony's grim prediction fresh in my mind, I could only hold his hand and hope and pray that he would make it.

When we arrived at Heathrow, he was again wheeled onto the food lift and as he was lowered to the ground, he caught sight of a group of distraught looking airport workers watching in total silence. He suddenly seemed to get a burst of adrenaline. He smiled and gave them a V sign they cheered, and we knew he was going to be alright. He was alright but never quite the same again. We made one final visit to France otherwise he spent his time between Chartwell and the London house near Hyde Park.

7

Growing Up

Today, growing up involves finding your direction in life: choosing your career, fulfilling your ambitions, finding happiness and security. Thankfully, this is now true for young men and young women alike. In the early sixties, however, most young women I knew were really just filling in time until they got married. I was no different.

Although my Churchillian heritage was steeped in politics and my father became secretary of state for Commonwealth Relations in 1960, I was not particularly interested in politics. In the years when he was negotiating the independence of almost a dozen British colonies, I was at first having fun, and then caught up in one drama unfolding after another.

These were the years when the Berlin Wall went up, Adolf Eichmann was hanged for wartime atrocities, *Private Eye* was launched and the Beatles single, 'Love Me Do' became their first hit. I was living every day as it came, and when it came with a challenge, I just got on with it.

When my parents divorced in 1960 after twenty-five years together, my father stayed in the Vincent Square house and my mother, Edwina and I all moved to Chester Row near Sloane Square. I do not remember being shattered or depressed about the break-up, and I certainly was not traumatised. In fact, Edwina and I were relieved as we did not like hearing the rows between them. I remember telling a girl at school that everyone's parents got divorced. My mother did not sit around all day moping, but we could see that she was not happy; She loved my father until the day she died.

In Chester Row, Edwina and I shared the top floor with Lukey, who lived-in, except at weekends when she would go off to a flat in Pimlico, only to come back to what she would call 'Black Monday' because all the washing-up was piled in the sink. We had no dishwasher, so when we ran out of plates, we went out to eat at the Brompton Grill. That was my mother's somewhat 'relaxed' approach to housekeeping!

I was certainly badly trained in the techniques of domesticity. When I lived at home, Lukey and Gray Gray did everything for me. Even after I started work at the General Trading Company, Lukey brought me my breakfast in bed and then I would run around the corner to work. Sometimes, when I had a romance going on, as soon as the post arrived, Gray-Gray would bring my letters to me at work. I do not think my mother ever had any idea about these special deliveries.

When I first started at the GTC, it was a lovely shop, which concentrated on wedding present lists about a hundred yards from Hyde Park Corner, behind where the Intercontinental Hotel is now. I was there for two or three months before we moved into new premises on Sloane Street.

It was there that I made a lifelong friend in Kristina Cronopulo who was ten years older than me. When she died, I found that she had kept my letters from the time that she went away for several months, in which I had written about the boyfriend of the moment. They are a dim memory now, but the letters make it clear that I fancied myself in love several times a month and took a lot of skiing holidays.

Kristina was rather senior at the GTC. She said she wanted me to help her set up the new kitchen department, but what did I know about kitchens? Nevertheless, we had great fun doing it together; we were very much doing our own thing, quite separate from everyone else working there. In effect, we ran our own upmarket little shop-within-a-shop. We stocked very nice things like the then-fashionable copper saucepans. Everyone loved our department, and I loved selling. I really enjoyed the challenge

One Christmas, a man walked in to do his Christmas shopping and ordered about twenty presents. He was faintly familiar, and I realised that I must know him, but did not have a clue who he was. He went around the whole shop ordering things, and then said, 'Send the bill to the office.' I said, 'Of course.' despite not having a notion where that might be. I dared not ask because, clearly, I was supposed to know!

I had to sift through all the cards he had given me, with names and addresses so that I could send on the various items, until I found an acquaintance I could ring up and ask, who he was. He was someone I had met at a party at the home of my friend, Mary Oppenheimer. He worked for Anglo-American and had sent Christmas presents to everyone. It was a lucky piece of detective work; the bill was huge.

For my twentieth birthday in May 1963, my father and stepmother, Marie Claire, gave a wonderful party for me at the house in a Vincent Square. Marie Claire liked doing things perfectly and perfection, in this case, did not come at the sort of price that my father would have understood. The food came from Fortnum and Mason and I wanted to have a West Indian band which was very popular at the time. We decided not to say how much it would cost for the evening as he might have been shocked by the fee which was ten pounds! I remember going to Harrods to buy some records to play in the band's breaks. I asked the assistant for a recommendation and he suggested, 'a new group called the Beatles who seem to be having some success.' The steel band and the Beatles were a great success and got everyone smooching and limbo dancing with equal enthusiasm.

During the next few months one drama followed another but everything paled into insignificance when, in October, tragedy struck, and my mother died from an overdose. She had suffered a number of breakdowns and was still depressed following her divorce from my father, who had remarried. I had gone to stay with a friend at his family house in Sussex. The following morning his mother came into my bedroom and told me that my mother had died, and that my aunt and uncle, Mary and Christopher Soames, who lived close by, were on their way to collect me and take me to London.

I do not think any of us articulated it, but we were not altogether surprised by our mother's death. Soon after our we got home the police arrived and wanted to see her bedroom. I spotted a pile of pills scattered on the floor and tried to cover them with my feet. Why I do not know but that was my instinctive reaction. Of course, they must have seen what I was doing but were too polite to comment.

We struggled through the cremation and a service at St Stephens Walbrook where poignantly my mother used to go every day to work as a volunteer for the Samaritans. The very moving service was led by Chad Varrah. The founder of the Samaritans.

I found myself living alone in my mother's house being looked after by the ever faithful Lukey and Gray Gray. The following weeks were to some extent blanked off in my mind. Two of my girlfriends came to stay and I went back to the General Trading Company. Understandably some people were awkward around me as they did not know what to say. On several occasions I saw someone I knew crossing the street to avoid having to commiserate. I stayed on for a bit at Chester Row but when, a few months later, I went to Kenya and then South Africa, the Chester Row house was sold, and that part of my life ended.

The same month as my mother died, my boyfriend, who was working for Jardine Matheson, the big British trading company in the Far East, dumped me. I had met him when he was halfway through six months leave. He was great fun and very attractive and I really believed that this was going to last. How could it when he lived halfway round the world?

His leave came to an end and he returned to Kuala Lumpur. After a few months I wrote and suggested that I would visit him. He replied that he was going to be travelling and it was not a good time. I said that if he did not want me, he should tell me. I did not want him to spare my feelings because of my mother's death. I sent a telegram saying, 'Please send me the answer regardless of the news.' He did exactly that. I was very upset but in the context of everything else it was hardly a disaster. It transpired that he had a live-in Chinese girlfriend all along. She was an experienced woman, I was a completely innocent girl.

I am sure that those of us who are old enough, know exactly where we were on the day that President Kennedy died. On 22 November 1963 I was having dinner with my grandfather at his London home in Hyde Park Gate. We had barely sat down for dinner when a television was placed on the table and we watched together as the dreadful story unfolded and history was made before our eyes. Tears poured down Grandpapa's cheeks as news came in that the young President had died. He cried again at the sight of his beautiful wife, still wearing her bloodstained pink suit, bravely watching the new President, Lyndon Johnson, being sworn in on Airforce One. The Kennedys seemed so young to everyone, but how young they must have looked to that old man approaching his ninetieth year. He was a very emotional man, and never afraid to show his tears. We were both crying. It is a moment I will never forget.

1963 had been a year full of drama, fun, romance, and sorrow. I had by force grown up a lot. But it was not yet over. The final weeks were to lay the foundations for my first big adventure and my life for the next six years.

r

8

White Mischief

In December 1963, not long after my mother died, my father, who was at the time secretary of state for the Colonies and for Commonwealth Relations, was due to go to Kenya and Zanzibar for their independence celebrations. In the normal course of events my stepmother, Marie Claire, would have gone with him, but she was pregnant and unable to travel. He asked me to accompany him.

I was already going to South Africa for Christmas to stay with my closest friend from school Mary Oppenheimer and this appeared to work perfectly both geographically and time wise. As I was going to be taken to Kenya courtesy of the British Government, I decided to use the money I would have spent on my ticket to South Africa on clothes for all the different events in Kenya and Zanzibar, a ball gown for the independence ball and the sort of formal outfits that I would never have needed in my normal life for lunches and dinners during the weeklong celebrations.

On the eve of our departure my father called and said, 'you can't go to South Africa from Nairobi. They will not like it because of Apartheid. So, you'd better come back with me, then go out again.' Horrified, I said, 'I can't do that because I can't afford the fare.' To which he said, 'But you were going to pay the fare anyway.' I said, 'I have spent the money on clothes.' To my surprise, he said that he would think of a way round it.

In 1963, Zanzibar was not a colony of Britain, but a protectorate, ruled by a sultan. This small island to the south of Kenya, close to the coast of Tanganyika, had been granted independence two years earlier but had remained under the protection of the United Kingdom. This status was relinquished two days before to coincide with Kenya's Independence Day.

As it turned out, soon after Zanzibar became independent, a bloody revolution led by a largely African faction, overthrew the new constitutional monarchy of the sultan and his Arab regime, and, within months, Zanzibar merged with Tanganyika as the new republic of Tanzania.

Oblivious to the history and the politics, I had an amazing time in Zanzibar. It was quite extraordinary. We stayed in Government House, a lovely building which was a fusion of Indian and Arab styles, right on the beach in the south west of the city. Prince Philip was there, my father, his number two, the minister of state for Commonwealth Relations, Andrew Cavendish, the eleventh duke of Devonshire, and me.

Andrew escorted me everywhere because I was doing all the things my stepmother, Marie Claire would have done. One event was tea with the sultana, the wife of the sultan of Zanzibar. It was a strange gathering, we sat and looked on in amazement as Her Majesty consumed a huge quantity of Cadbury's chocolate buttons served on gold plates. He also took me to the first souk I had ever been to and bought me my first pair of flip flops. This was the beginning of a nice friendship which lasted for the next twenty years.

In the evening, I could not resist the sight of the Indian Ocean. After a wonderful swim in the warmest sea I had ever been in I washed my hair and plugged in my curling tongs. To my horror all the lights in Government House went out. I had managed to fuse all the electrics in the entire building, and I had to go to the Independence celebrations with my hair sopping wet!

The next day we flew to Nairobi, where we again stayed at Government House, another splendid symbol of British imperial rule; a white-stucco, Palladian building with huge columns; the grandest house I had ever stayed in. The whole visit was one fascinating event after the other. I was awe-struck. I had only travelled a little in Europe, but this was Africa. I remember my father saying that Kenya was 'God's own country'. He was right. He and I escaped for a few days to Samburu game reserve. This was a rare experience for me to have him to myself and a memory that I cherish. I fell in love with Africa.

On Independence Day, 12 December, the ceremony took place in the Uhuru Stadium. In front of a huge crowd and amidst great pomp, Jomo Kenyatta was sworn in as the new prime minister of independent Kenya. An impressive looking man, with his famous red and black kofia hat and Masai flywhisk, he had been imprisoned by the British for eight years and only released in 1961. At first, he was feared by the white minority in Kenya, most of whom had wished that he had died during the Mau-Mau uprising that led to independence. However, by the end of his rule, in 1978, they hoped he would live forever.

Not surprisingly, much of the Independence Day festivities involved traditional tribal dancing. However, some petty bureaucrat must have decided that it would be unsuitable if the women dancers performed bare breasted in front of the British dignitaries. To spare any embarrassment they were all issued with Maidenform bras, not even black bras, but white ones. Whoever had made this ridiculous decision had made a huge mistake. It was as if the bras were fluorescent against their beautiful dark skin and in complete contrast to their gorgeous feather headdresses and ornately painted bodies. The result was much more indecent than if they had been left to dance as they always had.

Apart from the fact that we all got stuck in the mud getting there, the ball that evening was amazing, I was sitting watching when Kenyatta turned to me and asked me to dance. It was a symbolic gesture for him, as young though I was, I was, as my father's daughter, the senior British woman present. It was quite late, and we danced around for what seemed like an age. I was excited of course, but I had really been hoping to dance with Prince Philip.

Kenyatta was getting quite frustrated because they were going to sing, 'Maisha ya Mzee', Kenya's independence song and a tribute to him, and he had planned be on the dance floor at that moment but he had mistimed it and had got up an hour too early. We danced on and on until finally we got to the song. It was the longest dance I have ever had.

At lunch on the last day, I was sitting next to Prince Philip, when he said that he had heard that I was going to be staying on for a few days. When I confirmed that I was, he said he was going to go to a fishing camp on Lake Rudolph and would I like to go with him. As I opened my mouth to accept a voice from the other side of the table, his aide de camp, Admiral Christopher Bonham-Carter, who either had exceptional hearing, or could lip-read, said, 'Not suitable for women, Sir'. So that was that. My father would never have allowed me to go anyway.

Because of the Apartheid issue it was considered undiplomatic for me to go directly to South Africa therefore, so that the Kenyans would not know my final destination, my father had arranged for me to go on a staggered route staying with a couple of British high commissioners starting in Uganda. A telegram was sent to Kampala, saying, 'Minister's daughter arriving, look after her.'

How they must have cursed at the thought of entertaining me. They sent me off in an aeroplane to go and visit all sorts of places. Funnily enough, I ended up in a missionary's house where the wife was the sister of Miss Johnston who had been my art teacher at school. What a coincidence, right in the middle of Africa.

I went to see the Karamajong tribe in the north east, who are very tall like the Masai and have a similar ritual, where the men leap high into the air, in their 'adamu', their rite of passage dance. I wanted to take some photographs, but was told that was not a good idea, because they dance with no clothes on.

The next stop was Rhodesia, now Zimbabwe and the British High Commission in Salisbury, now called Harare. As I got off the plane, the high commissioner was waiting at the bottom of the steps. It was not Celia arriving, it was the minister's daughter. In the car on the way to his house he said, 'I don't know whether your father told you, I'm a bachelor.' Surprised that he thought this information in any way relevant I replied, 'No, I don't suppose he gave any thought to that.'

He was a very nice man called Jack Johnston. When we arrived at his house there was an elegant woman dressed in what were clearly designer clothes who appeared to be acting as the hostess. He introduced her, 'this is my housekeeper, Madame Schwartz.'

That night as we set off, all dressed up for a dance at the Rotary Club Madame Schwartz asked me to call her when I returned so she could help me get undressed. This surprised me as although my dress was quite elaborate it was not the sort that was difficult to take off. I declined her offer saying that I could manage on my own. After the dinner, when we arrived on the doorstep a huge insect flew down the front of my dress. I screamed and the high commissioner plunged his hand down my décolleté and, quick as a flash, pulled out the offending creature. The next morning, Madame Schwartz said 'What happened last night? I heard you cry out.' I said, 'Yes, an insect flew down the front of my dress, but Mr Johnson was wonderful. He fished it out.' When I saw the distressed expression on her face, I immediately realised that her role was much closer to the diplomat than that of a housekeeper.

On our way to the airport Mr Johnston said, 'You did not recognise Madame Schwartz, did you?' I replied, 'I have never seen her before, though my grandmother did once have a cook called Madame Schwartz.' At that moment, I understood what he was trying to tell me. I had last seen my grandmother's rather stout cook dressed in a starched white overall in the kitchen at Chartwell. She had now morphed into this elegant much slimmer jealous woman dressed in clothes straight from Paris. What an incredible coincidence.

When I eventually arrived in South Africa, I had a wonderful time. I had met Mary eight years before when we were at Heathfield, where she became my closest friend, and still is, despite the geographical void that separates us. She was the daughter of Harry Oppenheimer, the owner of de Beers and a very progressive politician. They lived in an enormous house, Brenthurst, in Parktown, a smart suburb of Johannesburg. Harry was a brilliant and captivating man who, far from feeling the need to impress anyone or show how clever he was, had the knack of making whoever he was speaking to feel that they were also intelligent and interesting.

Mary's mother Bridget was a force to be reckoned with. I liked her very much and got on well with her largely I think because I had known her so long and wasn't scared of her. She used to come to take us out from school and would ask where we wanted to go. One day we chose the ABC tea rooms in Windsor to have baked beans on toast. This was certainly a first for Bridget, but she did not bat an eyelid. Warren the chauffeur however was visibly shocked and embarrassed at having to park the Rolls Royce outside this very ordinary café and to wait for us outside standing self-consciously in his smart uniform.

I got to Brenthurst just in time for the Christmas parties. We had a lovely family Christmas which was followed by a Black and White Ball to celebrate Mary's twentieth birthday. The theme was chosen purely to dictate the colour scheme but would certainly not pass unnoticed in today's politically correct world. Bridget had taken us to have new dresses made for the occasion. Mary and I were shopping in Woolworths where she bought a diamanté tiara which she decided to wear for the party. It was clearly a joke but several of the guests admired it and assumed that it was her birthday present from her parents. This was a typical example of how if someone is expected to wear the real thing no one doubts it even in this case when it would have been very odd for a twenty-year-old to be wearing a diamond tiara at her birthday party.

The days after Christmas were not my finest hour. We went to a lunch party and I was asked what I wanted to drink. I never drank alcohol because I did not like the taste so settled on a tomato juice. It was a very hot day, so I drank a few and then began to feel distinctly odd. I had had three or four bloody Mary's and was very drunk. Mary took me home and put me to bed where I stayed all the next day. I have no idea what she said to her mother, but it was never discussed. Once I had recovered, we went to another party where determined not to make the same mistake I decided to play it completely safe and drink orange juice. Needless to say, after a few apparently innocuous glasses I was reeling. I had never heard of a Screwdriver! It was a tough way to learn about alcohol but certainly a useful lesson. I have never accepted a mixed drink since without seeing exactly what has gone into it.

We had a wonderful holiday at their ranch in Rhodesia where a delightful Irishman, naturally called Paddy, persuaded me, with typical blarney, that I would enjoy smoking if I started with menthol cigarettes. Indeed, I did and continued with the filthy habit for the next twenty years.

While I was in South Africa, it occurred to me that since I had arrived, I had never met a black person in a social setting. Mary, who was a liberal South African, arranged for us to have lunch with a friend of hers. To my surprise this was not as simple as I had thought. We had to go to a hotel in a special area, because of the stringent Apartheid laws. I was really shocked to see notices all over Johannesburg indicating whether street benches or public lavatories were for black or white people. Mary's friend was extremely nice, but I felt embarrassed that I had made an insensitive request.

Mary was in charge of the family charity and we went to Basutoland which, following independence, became Lesotho, in order that she could evaluate the projects of some prospective recipients.

In Basutoland, we were invited to lunch with the paramount chief, who later became King Moshoeshoe II of Lesotho. A very tall man, he had been at Ampleforth and Oxford University and acted just like an English country gentleman, an odd contrast amidst the timeless setting. I disgraced myself by spilling my Coca Cola all over the table.

We moved on to a monastery where we were to stay the night. We were entertained by the monks who played cards with us. Mary played bridge with the senior brothers and I played cheat with the younger ones. We had dinner with the brothers served by nuns from the nearby convent. We were then shown to two adjoining monastic cells and told that that the lights would go out shortly. In fact, they did, almost immediately, at which point various unholy expletives emanated from both of us as we stumbled around stubbing our toes in the dark.

While we were visiting the hopeful recipients of Mary's charitable fund, she was very definitely the 'grand lady' and I was the lady in waiting. At the next stop there was a reversal of roles as my father had arranged for us to stay with the resident commissioner, so I became, 'the minister's daughter and Mary the lady in waiting'! Yet again I disgraced myself when I let the bath overflow and it flooded the sitting room. Needless to say, they behaved as though I had done them a favour and given them an excuse to redecorate.

After a wonderful six weeks I went back to Government House in Nairobi. Following the independence celebrations, Malcolm MacDonald had invited me to visit them on my return journey to be company for his stepdaughter, Jane. I was not excited by the prospect, but my father had accepted the invitation on my behalf. Before I left Johannesburg, a friend had asked me what on earth I was going to do for two weeks at Government House. When I said I had no idea, he sent a telegram to a friend saying, 'Celia Sandys arriving. Look after her.'

When I arrived at Government House, the social secretary said, 'Michael Kennedy rang up and asked you to lunch and we accepted for you.' It transpired that Michael Kennedy's business partner, John Williams, was the one to whom the telegram had been sent. He was away, so Michael had opened it and decided that he would look after me. Lunch went well and he decided to make sure that I enjoyed my visit to Kenya. He was well practised at showing visitors around and, since he was in the tourist business, had no problem planning our tour.

Michael and John had an air charter company and two hotels one on the coast at Kilifi and a fishing camp on Lake Rudolph, the one that Prince Philip had told me about. He sent Jane and me there. It was a very beautiful place in an exotic setting with primitive thatched huts, long hours of drinking and playing a game called Cardinal Puff which was a bit like strip poker and big game fishing on the huge lake in an exotic setting near to the Ethiopian border. It is a very dangerous place now and was quite dangerous then.

I was meant to leave after two weeks, but Michael invited me to go and stay with him and his wife. I was in no hurry to go home. The house in Chester Row had been sold while I was away, there was no one waiting for me and a return to work at the General Trading Company was not very exciting compared to a few more weeks in Africa.

I happily accepted his invitation. Michael's wife, Jo, was an alcoholic who was out for the count by early evening most days. As a result of the years when the men were out chasing the Mau Mau during the Kenyan Emergency in the fifties many of the settlers' wives had become heavy drinkers. This is hardly surprising as while their husbands were out, they were left at home in fear of their lives. Their two older boys were at school in England and Nicky, their adorable eight-year-old daughter was at home. Once Jo was in bed Michael and I were thrown together and went out on the town.

He was twenty years older than me, I was used to being with much younger people, so it was fascinating to be with someone who knew his way around, was at ease with himself and very warm. Also, after the tragic death of my mother and the breakup with my boyfriend I subconsciously slipped into the protection of this kind and lovely man who was determined to give me a good time.

Michael had started his business after meeting John Williams on the ship going out to Kenya after the war. John had served in the RAF; Michael had been in the Army in Burma and they made friends and decided that they would go into business together.

Michael had a small inheritance from his mother who had invented the Kestos bra which was chosen as the standard supply for service women during the war. He and John ran through most of it trying to work out exactly what they were going to do.

They discovered that the Kenyan coffee mills, where the good coffee was sorted from the not-so-good, were not particularly efficient, and a lot of the good coffee was going to waste. They contracted to take away the waste, for which they developed a machine that filtered out the good coffee from the bad. After that breakthrough one thing led to another, an aeroplane to visit the coffee plantations, then Wilken Air, an air charter company and two hotels. By the time I got there, they had developed a profitable and fun business.

Michael took me to Mnarani Club their hotel on a creek that flowed into the Indian Ocean it was a lovely very laid-back place with a series of cabins on a cliff overlooking the sea. It was very popular with visitors from England who, wanting to avoid the cold winters, would return year after year to water-ski, go deep sea fishing or just to relax by the pool. He then he sent me off on safari with Maurice Coreth, an Austrian count who was a big game hunter. It was quite normal in Kenya for visitors to be passed around from person to person or from house to house. Everyone was incredibly welcoming, and I had a wonderful time unlike anything I had ever experienced. For the first time in my life I was completely free to do exactly as I wanted.

Maurice was on his own as his wife was in Ireland with their children. One day he said, 'Do you want to come elephant hunting?' Of course, I did I was having an amazing adventure. We had staff to look after us and we ate what Maurice shot. On one occasion I shot a buck for the pot and felt proud when we ate it for dinner. I had no taste for killing these beautiful animals so did not take it up. We slept in camp beds in the bush under the stars with nothing between us and the lions except mosquito nets.

Unlike my only previous camping experience in the South of France baths were no problem in the African bush. The man who filled my canvas bath had performed the same task for Ernest Hemingway. I did not think to ask if I was luxuriating in the same tub as the monkeys swung from tree to tree above my head. Maurice had been asked to cull an elephant that was causing trouble on the border of the game reserve. We went out with the trackers who gauged how far ahead the elephant was by plunging their arms deep in the droppings and feeling the temperature. He fired just a few feet away from the elephant as it came towards us ears flapping while I stood just behind him. Nobody thought anything was wrong with hunting then, now things are very different, and the elephant population is dwindling. Maurice, who died in 1997, would be horrified. Maurice worked hard to try to protect the endangered elephants and his son has carried on his work protecting the rhinos.

It was a crazy time. One day, I was asked to drive a Land Rover to Mombasa; 300 miles, at least half being a dirt track, which I was thrilled to do. Another time it was suggested that I have 'a bit of target practice', which meant shooting out the light bulbs. I was wide-eyed with amazement but having the time of my life.

Of course, everyone knew about the 'Happy Valley Set', a group of debauched, largely British and European aristocrats and adventurers, who settled near the Aberdare Mountains, drawn there by plentiful game for hunting and a life of luxury. In the 1930s and 40s they became infamous for their decadence and outrageous exploits, which included heavy drinking, habitual drug-taking and wild sexual promiscuity.

Diana Delamere was one of the central characters in the scandal known as 'White Mischief' after the title of the book by James Fox, and, later, the film of the same name. As Diana Coldwell, a very beautiful former model and bar manager in London, she moved to Kenya in late 1930, together with her new and much older husband, Sir John 'Jock' Delves Broughton.

She almost immediately began a very public affair with the unofficial leader of the expat community, Joss Hay, the earl of Erroll. She planned to divorce Broughton and marry Erroll, an arrangement to which Broughton is said to have given his reluctant blessing. When he had married Diana, he had apparently acknowledged that theirs was not, anyway on her side, a love match and told her that if she met someone else, he would understand and release her.

Erroll was discovered murdered in his car in January 1941. Broughton was charged with his murder but was acquitted in the trial. Ostracised by the Happy Valley Set, Broughton returned to England, where he committed suicide in a Liverpool hotel.

Diana married Gilbert Colville, one of the wealthiest and most powerful landowners in Kenya, in 1943 and inherited much of his fortune. She then married Tom Cholmondeley, the fourth Lord Delamere, vastly increasing her fortune. By the time of Delamere's death, in 1979, she was said to be the most powerful white woman in Africa, and called the, 'White Queen of Africa.' Diana had dazzling looks and a magnetic personality and although, by the time I met her, she was over fifty. She was still incredibly attractive, and it was easy to see how she had captured so many hearts.

Things had changed long before my arrival in Kenya, the excesses of White Mischief had gone but, for the white community, it was still an amazingly privileged life. Although many of the white farmers and settlers left with independence, those who stayed lived very well. By April 1964 Michael and I were going everywhere together, often on his Vespa. I was having a ball but could not stay for ever.

The high commissioner had tried to rein me in, but I had ignored him. I think it was difficult for him. On the one hand, I was still the minister's daughter, but on the other, I was this girl who was apparently running wild. One day I went to have lunch with him, and he asked what I planned to do next. When I told him that I was going back to England the following week, he said, 'I'm glad, if you weren't, I would have had to ask your father to call you home because people are talking about you.'

A week later, feeling despondent that my adventure was over, I was on my way home, travelling very comfortably, courtesy of the British government, in first class. The plane stopped to refuel in Rome. The man next to me got off and came back on with the *Daily Express* and said, 'You might like to read this.' He handed me the William Hickey column, in which my antics in Kenya were described in lurid detail: shooting out light bulbs and sitting on the counter in the men's bar in the very famous and very colonial Muthaiga Club.

The club is a legend. It opened in 1913 and became a watering hole for the British ruling elite in East Africa. Among the club's main founders was Berkeley Cole, an Anglo-Irish aristocrat and his brother-in-law, Hugh, the third Lord Delamere, who is regarded as the 'founding-father' of the white community in Kenya. Delamere was responsible for inviting out to Kenya to buy land, most of the rich settlers who became the Happy Valley Set. He was quite a character, notorious for riding his horse into the bar of the famous Norfolk Hotel in Nairobi and using its tables for jumping practice.

Muthaiga appears often in the literature of East Africa. Historian of colonial Africa, Caroline Elkins, describes the pink-stucco Club as, 'the Moulin Rouge of Africa', where, 'the elite drank champagne and pink gin for breakfast, played cards, danced through the night, and generally woke up with someone else's spouse in the morning.'

Muthaiga is also a prominent setting in the 1942 memoir of aviator Beryl Markham, 'West with the Night.' She described it very well:

> Its broad lounge, its bar, its dining-room, none so elaborately furnished as to make a rough-handed hunter pause at its door, nor yet so dowdy as to make a diamond pendant swing ill at ease, were rooms in which the people who made the Africa I knew danced and talked and laughed, hour after hour.

Beryl Markham was raised in Kenya and befriended, Karen Blixen and Denys Finch-Hatton, whose romance was described in Blixen's novel, *Out of Africa*. According to writer, Ulf Aschan, godson of Blixen's husband, Bror Blixen, 'The club had a rule, still in force, that a member is entitled to damage any loose property, as long as he pays double its value.'

With the *Daily Express* still under my arm, I got back to London, to find my father's private secretary waiting for me at the airport with a somewhat disconcerting greeting, 'I'm going to take you through customs and then the Minister wants to see you.' This was a surprise and not a pleasant one!

I was whisked straight off to the Commonwealth Office where Freda Smith, who had been my father's secretary for as long as I could remember, was waiting for me. Freda, who was known in the office as 'the faithful Miss Smith' whispered that he was not very pleased with me.

My father's office was enormous, full of paintings depicting Britain's imperial glories, huge ruby-red velvet curtains, a large marble fireplace and an array of plush leather chairs. He was sitting behind a huge walnut desk. I felt like a naughty child about to be berated by the headmistress. On the other hand, I was a grown woman, back from her first real adventure in life and had every intention of standing my ground.

I had no indelicate secret to hide; Amazingly I had returned to England as innocent as I was when I left but more worldly wise. The main reason for this was that I had no intention of getting pregnant but also because I still had a romantic expectation of the wedding night. It was 1964, the sexual revolution had barely begun, 'The Pill' had only just appeared from America and it was six years before Germaine Greer would write, *The Female Eunuch,* her ground-breaking book that transformed women's attitude to sex. Nevertheless, I knew that my wild and wonderful African adventure had involved behaviour that would have been unacceptable in England. I did however want to keep my relationship with Michael to myself for the time being.

'Sit down', were my father's opening words before he began the inquisition.

I have had some letters from Nairobi. One from a woman who said she saw you under the table in the dining room of Muthaiga Club and that since you did not appear to drink she assumed you must have been on drugs.

I responded confidently that I remembered the occasion perfectly: an old lady had dropped her bag and I went under the table to pick it up. I told him that I did not drink, and I did not take drugs. He persisted, 'Why are people complaining about you?' I replied, 'I don't know, but I did go on safari with a married man.'

My somewhat startled father asked, 'Did he go to bed with you?' I thought it best if in doubt to tell the truth, and said 'No.' 'What's wrong with the man' he asked, 'Is he queer or something?'

He was offended. He would have been offended if Maurice had slept with me, but, perversely, he was offended because he had not! A veil was drawn over the whole episode and that was the end of it. I said nothing at all about Michael Kennedy.

I was growing more independent. Homeless because my mother's house had been sold, I bought a seven-year lease on a small flat in Danvers Street, off the King's Road. it was the first place I had of my own. It cost me the princely sum of £750.

Michael came over to London that summer. He was still not divorced, but he and his wife were living apart and their children were at boarding school in England. We rented a flat and spent the summer together. That is when I introduced him to my father, who thought our proposed marriage was a very bad idea. He did not want me to get any more involved with a man who, on paper, was certainly an unfortunate choice: forty years old, almost twenty years my senior; two heart attacks; three children and a drunken wife. It did not look promising. If he and some of my friends had taken a more sympathetic line and not put me on the defensive, I might have been more cautious, and things might have turned out differently.

Michael flew backwards and forwards to Kenya, while I returned to the General Trading Company to mark time until he was free.

We spent Christmas in 1964 with Maurice and Ginny Coreth in Ireland. In January 1965, my grandfather died. In February, I sold my flat and my car and went off to Kenya and moved in with Michael, who was by then divorced. We rented a little cottage near Muthaiga Club where all our needs were looked after by Oganga. He was a wonderful cook but because the house was so small, he cooked, cleaned, and washed our clothes. I was in love with Michael and Africa and had nothing to go back to England for.

We came back to London and were married in October at the Caxton Hall in Westminster. Before the wedding, Edwina's husband, Piers Dixon, whose father was British ambassador in Paris, said, 'If you marry Michael, my parents will never invite you to the Embassy.' I replied that in that case he would not be welcome at my wedding. There was a big drama over that. Edwina did come, and so, eventually, did Piers.

My only sadness was that their recent deaths meant that neither my grandfather nor my mother were at the wedding, but my grandmother came with my two aunts Sarah and Mary. I planned the wedding with Marie Claire, my father's wonderful and beautiful new French wife. She was a great support to me, and we became good friends, a friendship that grew stronger and stronger over time. She is still one of the very most important people in my life. The guest list consisted mainly of my friends and family but also a considerable number of my father's political colleagues.

Like most girls I had dreamed of a beautiful white wedding dress but in the circumstances I wore a demure but pretty white dress and matching coat, from Belinda Bellville which I had chosen to suit whatever the weather brought forth. I certainly did not need the coat as the seventh of October was the hottest October day since records had begun.

Sarah went to Sydney Smith in the King's Road and bought the most amazingly theatrical purple velvet suit with a big black fox fur collar. It was extremely dramatic. Because of the hot day, she removed the fur collar, which left her suit with an indecently plunging neckline which revealed her white bra and completely destroyed the potential glamour of the outfit.

Between the wedding and the reception, at the Dorchester Hotel, Sarah visited every pub she could find along the way and had a drink to toast my marriage and her birthday which was on that day. If I had realised, I would have avoided that date as I would have known it was a recipe for disaster. By the time she got to the reception she was very drunk. Michael and I were receiving the guests with my father and Marie Claire. Sarah placed herself behind Marie Claire and as each guest came forward, she shot out her hand saying, 'I'm representing Diana who unfortunately could not be with us today.' My father was furious, Marie Claire devastated, the guests dumbfounded. I was the only one who could smile at the behaviour of my enchanting but impossible aunt. Her sister, Mary, stepped in and ushered her out of the hotel where they had a very public row on an island in the middle of Park Lane. After a fabulous honeymoon in Antigua and Barbados we returned to Kenya by sea and settled into our new home.

During my married life with Michael in Kenya, I never thought about money. Everything seemed to be covered by company expenses. I was in Kenya for five years and when I left, I still could not cook. Everything was done for me; I could not do simple domestic things, but I could have run an embassy. We had a lovely Spanish-style house, which seemed to run perfectly. We had a charmed life, looked after by an incredible staff. Oganga was in charge of the kitchen, Clement combined the roles of butler and lady's maid and a younger man assisted them in the most menial tasks. The gardener was officially called Wellington but inevitably became known as The Boot.

In 1966, I became pregnant. The initial excitement soon changed to anxiety. I was constantly in pain for which my only relief was neat vodka, I would keep a bottle by the bed. I knew something was not right and not trusting the local doctors, (one of my friends had just had a baby and the doctor had given her a hysterectomy at the same time without consulting her) I went to London, where I miscarried, which was a very distressing experience. Happily, Justin was born the following year and when he arrived, we hired a Swedish baroness, who had fallen on hard times, to be our Nanny.

I dressed the staff in beautiful white uniforms with gold epaulettes and gave them white gloves to wear. They were thrilled because they thought they were the smartest staff outside Government House in the whole of Nairobi. I bought them European beds and gave them curtains in their rooms. I was faced with a delicate problem. How to ask them to use deodorant without offending them. I solved it by giving them each a Mum roulette the same as mine. Some of our friends were upset because they thought their staff would want to be treated in the same way.

Michael's children were at boarding school in England but came back for the holidays. His two sons, who quite naturally, felt sorry for their mother, could not bear me, the oldest was only eight years younger than me, but I got on really well with his daughter, Nicky. It was difficult. I remember once, staying in a house on the beach where the walls were not very thick, and hearing them say, 'We must make her go away' Fortunately, it all settled down and we got the children under control and we all got along quite well.

As Michael and his partner, John Williams, had an air charter company and two hotels we flew everywhere in the planes and stayed in the hotels. It was all great fun. Our friends came to stay so we were never bored. England was only eight hours away and because we were in the tourist business, we could get especially cheap tickets for as little as £20. Edwina would call from London, which was by then the centre of the 'swinging sixties', and say, 'I'm having a party tomorrow; do you want to come?' So, I would jump on a plane.

I enjoyed several experiences which I suppose you could call, 'Out of Africa' moments. Denys Finch Hatton and Karen Blixen were long gone of course, and I certainly did not bump into Robert Redford or Meryl Streep, but I did meet two fascinating 'white hunters', who could readily have been cast in the famous film. One was a charming Irishman called Liam Lynn and his Austrian partner, Prince Alfie von Auersperg.

Alfie was divorcing his wife, wealthy American, Sonny Crawford, and was doing very well financially in the settlement. Sonny was soon to re-marry Claus von Bulow, and then became, in tragic and mysterious circumstances, the infamous, 'Sleeping Beauty'.

In 1980, as a result of either hypoglycaemia, or what was alleged to have been an overdose of insulin, she was left, barely alive, in a non-responsive coma. Von Bulow was accused of murdering Sonny for her vast family fortune and was convicted, before being later acquitted in a re-trial. Sonny never recovered and died in 2008. In a settlement with Sonny's family in 1987, Claus agreed to divorce Sonny and be disinherited from her will. More than thirty years on he is still alive and in his nineties.

Although Alfie was a prince of a very ancient Central European royal family, he had not had much money before meeting Sonny. He had met her at a hotel in Austria, where he was a tennis coach. They had two children together.

Soon after I met Liam and Alfie, who was probably the most beautiful man I have ever seen, we worked an arrangement which was very satisfactory for us all. Every year I used to give big party <u>but</u> at their suggestion, I agreed to turn it into an extravaganza, in their honour, so that they could impress their top clients when they arrived in Nairobi to go big game hunting. In exchange, they gave me a week's safari for me and my friends. I would have given the party anyway, but the wonderful safaris were a great bonus.

Liam would sing Irish sings around the campfire while Alfie would just look beautiful, we had so much fun. While writing this book I suddenly got the idea that I would like to find Liam. I knew that Alfie had died but thought there was a chance that Liam was still alive.

I googled him and to my excitement I discovered that Liam Lynn had a garage near Dublin. It was the weekend, so I contained my excitement until Monday and called the Dublin number and was put through to Liam Lynn. I went straight to the point announcing myself fifty years after our last meeting. There was a pregnant pause and the Irish voice said, 'I am Liam Lynn, but I think it is my uncle that you want. Unfortunately, he died thirty-eight years ago.' Very disappointing but this confirmed the advice I was given when I started writing to always, 'interview the oldest witnesses first.'

One of my few regrets in Kenya was that I did not learn to fly. It would have been so easy because Michael and a John had their own aeroplanes. Sadly, I never got around to it. Accompanied by the perfect melody of John Barry's music, just as Robert Redford and Meryl Streep did in that wonderful sequence in their movie, I could have flown over the Mara, scattering wildebeest, and putting pink flamingos to flight.

Michael and I were together for five years. I was contented but I knew it was not going to last. I just knew it was not really right. I was too young. The time came when I realised this. So, when I visited London, I would always go with Justin under my arm, just in case I did not go back.

I remember a friend of mine, who got married very young, straight from school, and ran away, because she knew it was not going to work. At the time I thought it very brave and I suppose that may have influenced me. It was not that I had fallen out with Michael, I had not. I had fallen out of love with him. I just did not want to get into a situation where we were enemies. Little by little our relationship broke down. We never had a row. Perhaps that was the problem.

We went on a skiing holiday to Courchevel then on to Val d'Isere where Edwina joined us. 'This is Brad' she said, with an air of innocence when she arrived with an attractive man on her arm, 'Isn't it funny? We were on the same plane, going to the same place. He rented a car and gave me a lift.'

Having no guilty conscience, I could be very friendly with Brad, whom I had met before. Michael however saw it differently and accused me of importing my boyfriend. I was furious and packed my bags and set off to London. An hour after I left there was an avalanche and Val d'Isere was cut off for five days. That evening, Michael went to tell Edwina it was time for dinner. He knocked on her door, walked in and found her in bed with Brad. He realised he had made a big mistake.

Meanwhile, I had arrived back at Edwina's house in London. Her husband, Piers, was there with a disapproving Nanny. There were a lot of half-empty champagne bottles in the fridge. He had obviously been having a few parties for two!

Eventually Michael came back to London and we had a show down which resulted in him going back to Kenya. I stayed in London and effectively never went back. And that was more or less the end of it. I did not want to hang on and make us both miserable when I knew it was futile. I was sad but knew it was not going to last. Michael was devastated.

I stayed close to Nicky who by then was at school in England. A few years later she became pregnant and came to London to have the baby. She came to see me on her way to the airport and put her head out of the taxi window and said, 'If anything happens to me, I have left you Sasha.' This was perhaps the biggest compliment that anyone had paid me. I watched her drive off with tears in my eyes. She later married and with her Swedish husband had a son. Tragically she committed suicide at an addiction clinic in Bristol a few years later.

9

The Passing of a Legend

The American author, Ted Morgan, one of my grandfather's many biographers, called his study of Winston's early life, *A Young Man in a Hurry*. It is a perceptive title. From an early age, Churchill was convinced that it was his destiny, 'to do something in the world'. But he sensed that he had to get on with it, fearing that, like his father, who died at the age of 45, he would be cut off in his prime and denied his destiny.

This was a constant preoccupation in his early years. From prison in South Africa, on 30 November 1899, he wrote to his friend, the prince of Wales, 'I am twenty-five today, so little time remains.' Fifty years on, speaking at the Mansion House, he celebrated his seventy-fifth birthday with the declaration, 'I am ready to meet my Maker. Whether my Maker is prepared for the great ordeal of meeting me is another matter.' Fifteen years would elapse before that final meeting would take place.

Thankfully, those years made it possible for me to get to know my grandfather really well. I have happy and treasured memories of time spent with him at Chartwell, Chequers and Hyde Park Gate, travelling with him with him on painting holidays in the South of France and on the amazing cruise on the Onassis yacht.

When the family gathered to celebrate his ninetieth birthday in November 1964, the unspoken thought in everyone's mind was that the

Above left: My maternal grandparents, Winston and Clementine Churchill, on the Thames during the war.

Above right: My paternal grandparents, Mildred and George Sandys. They were married in 1905, the photograph was probably taken at that time.

Right: A family gathering at Chequers 1942, the year before my birth. Clementine, Winston and my mother, Diana, are at the front. My aunts, Mary and Sarah, are behind my grandparents. My father, Duncan Sandys, is behind my mother. Peregrine and Johnny Churchill at the back, my grandfather's nephews.

My aunt, Sarah, with my grandfather at the Tehran Conference, 28 November 1943. She acted as his as his aide-de-camp at the meetings between the 'Big Three' when I was just six months old. Sarah had impressed Roosevelt at Tehran, prompting him to bring his own daughter Anna to Yalta as his aide-de-camp.

Stalin shaking Sarah's hand at the Tehran Conference.

Above left: My mother. This photograph may well be from 1932, the year she married her first husband, John Milner Bailey.

Above right: My parents at the coronation 1953.

Above left: Aged six months 1943.

Above right: Dominic with my grandmother 1971.

Above: My christening with brother Julian and sister Edwina, 29 June 1943.

Below left: On my mother's knee with Julian and Edwina 1945.

Below right: With Nanny Buckles, Trafalgar Square 1946/47.

Above: With my mother at Vincent Square 1946/47.

Below left: My favourite animal, Bully Face, at Furze Down, Hampshire 1946/47.

Below right: With Nanny Buckles, , my grandmother Mildred and Edwina 1946/47.

Above left: Vincent Square 1948.

Above right: Trafalgar Square 1949.

Below left: My favourite (yellow) dress 1950.

Below right: My father had been made minister of supply in Churchill's new government. My mother and I met him at the airport on 29 April 1954 after he flew in from Canada.

A still of *Royal Wedding*, my aunt, Sarah, with Fred Astaire (1951). It was her most successful film and she played the role of Anne Ashmond.

Above left: My aunt, Sarah, with her second husband Anthony Beauchamp, at a New Year's Eve party at El Morocco nightclub, New York City, 1951. I did not like him. He was often quite nasty to Sarah and killed himself with an overdose of barbiturates in 1957.

Above right: Following Anthony's death, Sarah developed a drinking problem, and was arrested several times and charged with public drunkenness. On 13 January 1958 she was taken into custody in Los Angeles.

Above left: With my mother at a clinic in Italy, where she was recovering from a nervous breakdown, 1953.

Above right: My aunt, Sarah in 1962 at the time of her third marriage, this time to Lord Audley, the love of her life. His death, just fifteen months after their wedding, left her devastated.

Below: Croquet with my grandmother and my mother, at Chartwell 1961.

Above: The *Christina*, Aristotle Onassis' extraordinary yacht, July 1959.

Right: I was probably more impressed with the private seaplane on the top deck and the seawater swimming pool with a mosaic-tiled floor.

Above: Christina 'Tina' Onassis sitting by the pool, this time with sea water in it. She divorced Onassis in 1960 after discovering about his affair with Callas. She and her two children by Onassis all died tragically. Her son Alexander died in a plane crash in 1973. Tina was found dead in a hotel suite in Paris on 10 October 1974. The body of her daughter Christina was found by her maid in the bathtub of a mansion in Buenos Aires, 19 November 1988.

Below: My mother watching Ari and my grandfather playing bezique.

Right: Maria Callas in conversation while Winston and Clementine relax in the background. Just five weeks after this first visit to the Christina with her husband Giovanni Battista Meneghini, Maria recorded one of her most famous operas, La Gioconda, by Amilcare Ponchielli at Teatro alla Scala in Milan.

Below: Ari and Winston in the pool. It was dry and had been lowered, presumably to lessen the effect of sea breezes.

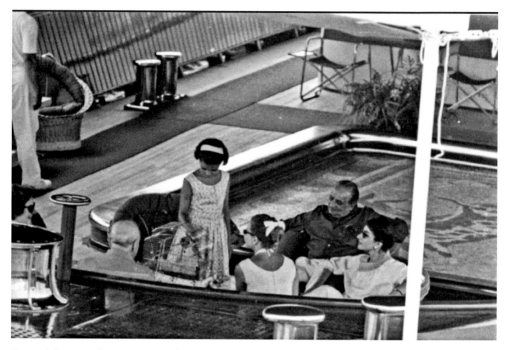

From left to right: Winston, Christina Onassis (aged 9), Tina, Giovanni and Maria. Christina seems fascinated by my grandfather's pet budgerigar, 'Toby'.

A photograph taken at the same time, probably by a paparazzo with telescopic lens from the shore. *From left to right*: Ari, unknown man and woman, Tina, Maria, and Giovanni.

Leaving the Hotel de Paris, Winston with Onassis on his left and Sergeant Murray (his bodyguard) on his right. Anthony Montague Browne directly behind.

Dinner at the Casino. I am on my grandfather's right, then Nonie Montague Brown. I don't remember who the man was. Maria is listening to Winston with interest, on his left is Tina, and Ari semi-veiled behind the curtain.

27 July 1959, Portofino: 'My grandparents stayed on deck, waving off the women, as we set off for a tour around the town. Tina was once again beautifully turned out. Even though I felt I passed muster, I took one look at her understated chic and realised that she was perfectly dressed. By contrast Callas by day seemed to get it entirely wrong. She wore a garishly coloured floral jumpsuit that could have been run up from chintz curtains and became increasingly awkward and irritable as we were followed everywhere by paparazzi.' (*Keystone Pictures USA*)

The calm before the storm, Maria and Tina at Delphi, Thursday 30 July 1959. Within one year both would be divorced in the one of the most media-covered celebrity scandals of the twentieth century.

The same day at Delphi, with my grandmother, Clementine. On the right is Anthony Montague Browne, my grandfather's private secretary with Callas and Tina.

With Ari's wife, Tina, at the Miramare Hotel, Rhodes, August 1959.

With my grandfather, early 1960s.

Above left: With my grandfather in the hills above Monte Carlo.

Above right: South of France, 1962, with Nonie and Anthony Montague Browne and my grandfather.

Above: After breaking his hip in the Hotel de Paris in Monaco in June 1962, Anthony Montague Browne and I flew back with him to Heathrow on an RAF plane sent by Prime Minister, Harold Macmillan. I am on the extreme right of the photo, with Anthony behind my grandfather. My uncle Randolph is to Anthony's left.

Right: My father was secretary of state for Commonwealth relations and, as his daughter, I was the senior British woman at Kenya's Independence Ball, so Kenyatta asked me for the first dance. I wasn't really as startled as I look in the photograph.

Below: 12 December 1963. Independence Day for Kenya. Prince Philip is standing with Kenya's new prime minister, Jomo Kenyatta.

Giving Grandpapa a kiss on the cheek.

My fatfather accompanies me on wedding day at Caxton Hall Westminster in October 1965. It was my first marriage, to Michael Kennedy, a British/Kenyan entrepreneur.

Right: With cameras and reporters everywhere, I arrive to see my ailing grandfather at his home at Hyde Park Gate on 16 January 1965.

Below: My grandfather's flag-draped coffin is carried by Grenadier Guards into St Paul's Cathedral for the funeral service.

Above: In the coffin's wake, once more carried on the shoulders of the bearer party, we processed up the steps and into the cathedral in strict order of family seniority.

Left: My father at 10 Downing Street with Prime Minister, Sir Alec Douglas Home and Ian Smith, Prime Minister of Southern Rhodesia. This was one decolonisation that did not go smoothly. The Unilateral Declaration of Independence (UDI) was a statement adopted by the Cabinet of Rhodesia on 11 November 1965, resulting in an international diplomatic incident.

My aunt, Sarah, 1966. Following the tragic death in Granada, Spain, of her husband, Lord Audley, from a heart attack, on 3 July 1963, Sarah's life quickly deteriorated. He was the love of her life and they were very happy. The death was a shock as he was only 49.

Campaigning for the June 1970 general election with my second husband, MP for Westbury, Dennis Walters, and his daughter, Lorian.

My company car and my pride and joy, a white Triumph Stag, 1976.

'Gorgeous' Gianni, in full Highland regalia, Scotland.

Family

Above left: My eldest, son Justin, 1967.

Above right: Justin and Dominic 1974.

'My four children captured at around the same age'

Justin.

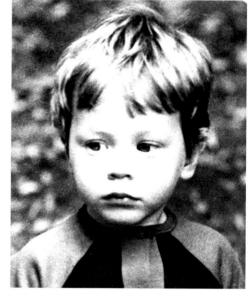

Dominic.

Alexander.

Sophie.

Right: My third husband, Ken Perkins 1982.

Below: My great friend Robert Hardy entertaining us at Alexander's christening, 1986. Ken is to the left, my sister Edwina's son, Hugo Dixon, is to the right.

Married bliss with Ken, Alexander and Sophie, Bampton, Devon, 1989.

Still living the good life, 1991.

With my aunt, Mary Soames, in sunny climes, *circa* 2008.

Above left: Sophie's wedding, 2018.

Above right: The happy brood 2018.

Alexander with Justin's family: wife, Paula, who died in (2019) and sons, Archie and Max, 2018.

Above left: A mid 90s portrait.

Above right: Not family, but my very close friend—Mary Oppenheimer. We first met at Heathfield School and remained good friends ever after. I frequently visit her in South Africa.

'The Great and the Good'

With Margaret Thatcher at the Churchill War Rooms, December 1999.

With Ted Heath at the Churchill War Rooms, December 1999.

With Fidel Castro, Cuba, September 2000.

With 103-year-old Gregorio Fuentes, on whom Ernest Hemingway had based his 1952 novel, *The Old Man and the Sea*.

Above: With George W. Bush at the White House, 2002.

Right: With Lady Williams of Elvel, who as Jane Portal served as secretary to Winston Churchill from 1949 to 1955.

'Tours and TV'

My South African Tours began in 1999. Here local historian, Ken Gillings, is describing the famous Boer War incident in November 1899 when the military train carrying my grandfather was derailed in a Boer ambush.

Guided by famous South African historian David Rattray, we're on Spion Kop, where 243 British soldiers were killed under Boer gunfire on 24 January 1900.

fateful meeting with his Maker could not be long delayed. Although I remember that he smiled benignly throughout the evening, I am sure he knew it too.

My grandfather's birthdays were always heralded by a flurry of comings and goings: telegrams, cards, letters and flowers would flood in from all over the world and for this particularly auspicious celebration there were more than 70,000, as well as the usual magnificent cake from Madame Floris's bakery in Soho.

Her creation was, as ever, beautifully decorated with a Churchillian theme, garlanded with oak leaves and a plaque quoting, 'In war resolution, in defeat defiance, in victory magnanimity, in peace goodwill.' It took two men to manoeuvre it through the front door of my grandparents' house at Hyde Park Gate, a quiet cul-de-sac on the south side of the Park.

Outside the house, a crowd of well-wishers and photographers had gathered, along with a small group of serenading musicians, all waiting patiently in the hope of catching a glimpse of him. On that day, wearing his velvet siren suit in what was probably the last photograph ever taken of him, he waved to the crowds from the window. He looked very old, but gave a warm, serene smile.

The dress code for these birthday parties was always black tie. As usual Grandpapa wore one of the many siren suits that Turnbull & Asser had been making for him in navy blue, bottle green and burgundy velvet since the war with velvet slippers with WSC embroidered in gold.

My grandmother usually wore what was called a hostess gown, the most luxurious and glamorous dressing gown of watered silk, which she could have worn to a dance. She wore this over her nightdress, though as she was always fully made up and wearing her jewellery, she cannot have saved much time getting ready for bed.

After toasting my grandfather in his favourite Pol Roger champagne in the drawing room, we went down to the beautiful dining room with its huge Persian carpet and silk striped chairs. Grandpapa, who had not been able to manage the stairs for some time, made a majestic descent in the lift, a golden cage-like contraption, which had been installed so that he could have dignified access to the garden and the dining room.

I do not remember it as the most cheery of dinners. My grandfather had been getting gradually frailer over the previous few years. Although unhappy that he would no longer be with us, we could not be sad for him. For some time, he had been tired of living and was more than ready to go. He had been increasingly withdrawing from life, especially after he lost the solace of painting. Conversation dwindled as he seemed to retreat into himself.

He used to sit in his chair staring at the fire, or at the dining room table, puffing at his cigar and sipping his brandy. Just when we thought he had sunk into his own world, he would look up, give his puckish smile, and say something totally relevant to the general conversation.

Companionship was always important to him and he was always happy to be given a kiss, to hold hands and to exchange 'wows' with his nearest and dearest. 'Wow' was the family cry that he and Clementine had invented and that we, his children, and grandchildren, had inherited. It could be spoken with different intonations at moments of joy or sorrow, but always with love. There was a lot of *wowing* around the table that night.

Our small family group at that last birthday dinner comprised: my uncle, Randolph, with his children, Winston and Arabella: my aunts, Sarah and Mary with her husband, Christopher Soames; my brother, Julian and sister, Edwina, with her husband Piers Dixon; my grandmother's cousin, Sylvia Henley and me. The only other guests were Jock and Meg Colville and Anthony and Nonie Montague Browne. Both couples were close and trusted family friends. Jock had been my grandfather's private secretary both during the war and during his second premiership in the early fifties. Anthony had been seconded to Churchill from the Foreign Office in 1952 and stayed with him until his death. He really did become part of the family. We all confided in him and he was custodian of all the family secrets.

I was sitting between Anthony and Christopher Soames. For some reason, maybe to lift the mood, I disclosed the secret that was foremost in my mind: once he was free, I was going to marry Michael Kennedy, a still-married man twice my age, I think I must have been in the mood to confide. It could not have been the drink speaking, as I hardly touched alcohol, apart from an occasional vodka and bitter lemon. Perhaps I wanted to stir things up and shock a little, or perhaps I just wanted the secret to be out. I could see surprise and disapproval written on their faces, and, after a short pause while they digested the news, they said, almost in unison, 'He's the same age as us!' I realised then that this was a foretaste of the reaction I would get from others when I told them of my plans.

I do not think I cared either way whether they were in favour of my choice or not. I did not consider I needed their approval. I certainly had no illusions that this was a suitable match. Yet, the more people who said it was unsuitable, the more determined I became.

I remember telling my father that he could say what he liked before he met Michael, but if he criticised him after that, he would not see me again. He was speechless and very displeased. The day before I got married, my father's solicitor rang to tell me my father was asking what sort of settlement Michael was going to make on me. I said, thinking on my feet, that he was going to match pound for pound whatever my father settled on me. The answer of course was nothing. I was not hurt, because I knew my father had not planned any provision. But I thought it was very clumsily done, and I was pleased with my reply.

The evening ended early, but my cousin Winston and I were in no mood to go home. His wife, Minnie, was expecting their first child and, because of complications, was in hospital and Michael had just returned to Kenya after spending Christmas with me in London. So, to raise our spirits, we set off for Annabel's, and danced the night away.

Six weeks later, on 11 January 1965, my grandfather suffered a massive stroke and never left his bed again. Soon afterwards, Anthony Montague Browne telephoned to tell me that my Aunt Sarah was arriving from Rome early the next morning and to ask if I could collect her from the airport and have her to stay at my flat. It only took me twenty minutes to get from the flat in Chelsea to Heathrow in the early hours of the morning.

That was the easy bit. I found Sarah being mobbed by journalists and photographers who had heard that Grandpapa was not well. We finally got away and went straight to Hyde Park Gate where, once again, crowds of distraught well-wishers, reporters and cameramen gathered outside the house in response to the news. They all behaved with great respect and waited patiently for the regular bulletins issued by his doctor, Lord Moran.

There was no doubt that my grandfather was dying, and we could only wait for nature to take its course. He had had a massive stroke and it was clear that the end was near. Little by little over the following nine days, with his beloved marmalade cat curled up by his side, he sank into a deeper and deeper sleep. I went to see him every day and the cat was always in the same position. My grandmother was magnificent. She sat by his bed holding his hand for hours and only left the house when my Aunt Mary insisted on taking her for a walk in the park.

Sarah and I went backwards and forwards between Hyde Park Gate and my very small flat on Danvers Street. Sarah was the most attractive and talented of my grandparents' children, but never fulfilled her potential. With the not inconsiderable help of her first two husbands, over time she had become an alcoholic.

Having witnessed Sarah's close relationship with the bottle for as long as I could remember, I knew that drink was going to compound the difficulties of this particular time. What I had not accounted for was Katie, Sarah's Irish maid, who had been her dresser in the theatre. Katie was a delightful woman, but she shared Sarah's fondness for alcohol. Before I left for the airport to collect my aunt, I poured all the alcohol in the flat down the sink. This precaution was to no avail.

Katie's principal role was not mistress of the wardrobe or bedroom, but 'procurer of hard liquor'. She found more hiding places than I could keep up with! I found bottles everywhere, even in the cistern of the loo. Trying to keep Sarah sober was always an uphill battle, but if ever there was cause to resort to drink, this was it. On some days, when I saw the danger signals, I hurried her to Hyde Park Gate before she was too far gone, so that at least she could be spared any public humiliation.

On two occasions, the telephone rang early in the morning and we were summoned because Grandpapa's condition was deteriorating. They were both false alarms, but he was sinking all too obviously. One day, after our visit, we were due to have lunch with my sister, Edwina, at her house. I was feeling very stressed from the strain of trying to keep Sarah sober. Not wanting to drink in front of her, I took a bottle into the bathroom to dose myself with medicinal vodka. Feeling much better, we sat down for lunch, but I had forgotten the vodka in the bathroom. Sometime later, I realised that Sarah had vanished. I found her in the bathroom, very much the worse for wear, the empty bottle in her hand.

A few years before, Grandpapa had said that he would die on the same date as his father's death. It was an uncannily portentous prediction. During those long anxious days, among all the many concerned calls, was one from Sir Michael Adeane, the queen's private secretary, enquiring how he was. Anthony Montague Browne told me that he had replied, 'He will go on for a few more days. He once said he would die on the 24th of January.' That must have given rise to a strange conversation at Buckingham Palace.

On the 20th, Lord Moran issued a bulletin, 'The weakness of Sir Winston's circulation is more marked.' On the 22nd, he issued another, 'Sir Winston has had a restful day, but there has been some deterioration in his condition.' And on the 23rd, 'The deterioration of Sir Winston's condition is more marked.'

About six thirty on the morning of 24 January 1965 we got the summons. This time it was not a false alarm. We threw on our clothes and drove to Hyde Park Gate as fast as my mini could take us.

As usual, with his faithful cat still curled up next to him, we found my grandfather sleeping peacefully. Grandmama was sitting beside him holding his hand, with Randolph and Winston standing on the other side. Sarah, Mary, and I knelt at the foot of the bed and reached out to hold hands. Lord Moran hovered beside him and I was vaguely aware that Roy Howells, the nurse who, in the guise of his valet, had been caring for him with discretion and tenderness for several years, the other duty nurse and Anthony had also sunk to their knees behind us.

It was hard to imagine that this frail old man, whose existence was ebbing away, had lived such a tumultuous and extraordinary life. It seemed as though we were all holding our breath so that we could hear his failing gasps for as long as possible. After a short while, he sighed two or three times; then there was silence. We all knew what it meant; no one moved; no one spoke.

My grandmother looked at Lord Moran and asked, 'Has he gone?' He just nodded.

Perhaps he had willed it, but my grandfather had managed to make his remarkable prediction come to pass. On 24 January 1965, seventy years to the day, and almost to the minute, since his father, Lord Randolph, had died, Winston Leonard Spencer Churchill slipped away to meet his Maker.

We were all relieved for him, that his long journey was at an end, but distraught that he was gone, and shaken at the realisation that the man who had been at the core of all our lives for what seemed like forever, was no longer with us.

He left me with one last gift: I had always been frightened of death, though I had never encountered it before; but the sight of his peaceful end, surrounded by his family, and with his beloved cat at his side, removed all fear.

After a few moments of private thought, prayer or reflection, we gave him a final kiss and moved slowly into the dining room where we sat down to a subdued breakfast while the bulletin was posted, 'Shortly after 8.0 clock this morning. Sunday, January 24th, Sir Winston Churchill died at his London home. Moran.' The radio was placed on the table and we listened as the news was broadcast to the world.

I went to Matins at Chelsea Old Church that day and got my first glimpse of the country's public grief on the streets and in the congregation. From there I drove to my father's house. It was his birthday, and the former prime minister, Alec Douglas Home, joined us for a sombre and reflective lunch.

The queen had long before made the decision that her first prime minister should be given a lying-in-state and a state funeral. This was the first time that such an honour had been granted to a commoner since Gladstone in 1898. A few years earlier, I had been told by a boyfriend, who was in the army, that they had been rehearsing for his funeral, which had been code named 'Operation Hope Not.'

London was in a state of shock, nowhere more so than among the crowds of people, from all over the country and abroad, queuing for the lying-in-state at Westminster Hall. It was freezing January weather, but no one complained as, hour after hour, 300,000 people queued along the damp pavements of the Embankment and over the bridges of the Thames. The mood was incredibly solemn as they shuffled forward in reverential silence.

We were allowed to enter by a side door. I went every day late in the evening. Each time I was greatly moved by the sight of the coffin, covered by the Union Jack with the Order of the Garter lying on it. It was guarded by four household cavalry officers standing motionless at each corner of the coffin, heads bowed, the candlelight flickering in their gleaming breastplates.

I stood watching the seemingly endless stream of silent and dignified people slowly making their way past the catafalque, I felt profoundly sad and enormously proud. I was sad that he was no longer with us, but proud of all that he had done to deserve the gratitude, affection and admiration of the people who had braved the freezing weather to honour him.

The tributes to his life flowed like a torrent. General de Gaulle, president of France, a staunch ally, and equally constant adversary, sent a letter to the queen in which he wrote, 'In the great drama, he was the greatest of all.' Clement Attlee, his deputy prime minister during the war and his successor, said of him, 'He had sympathy, incredibly wide sympathy for ordinary people all over the world. We have lost the greatest Englishman of our time; I think the greatest citizen of the world of our time.'

The funeral took place six days after his death on 30 January. Once the family had assembled in Westminster Hall, the bearer party of the Grenadier Guards carried the coffin to Palace Yard where it was placed on the gun carriage. The procession moved off, the men of the family walking behind the gun carriage, which was pulled by naval ratings, the women riding in five of the queen's carriages.

Riding in the first carriage, was my grandmother, wearing a long black veil, which was very glamorous and slightly mysterious, and my two aunts, Sarah, and Mary. My sister, Edwina, and I, with rugs tucked round us and hot bricks at our feet, rode in the second. By strange coincidence, Sarah, Mary, Edwina, and I had all bought practically identical black fox fur hats, which although well suited to the bitterly cold day made us look as if we were in uniform.

At nine forty-five, Big Ben sounded for the last time that day and the gun carriage moved off. From that moment, it was if we were taking part in an astonishing pageant. The script had been written some years earlier and rehearsed to perfection by all the official participants. We however had received no instructions so, as though in a trance, we followed the person in front.

However, we had to be careful. No matter how sad one is feeling, it is almost impossible to avoid showing warmth when speaking to someone you love. Edwina and I decided that we would not speak on the journey, lest even the shadow of a smile gave the wrong impression to the crowd, or an eagle-eyed photographer. From time to time we squeezed each other's hands, but that was all.

As our carriage swayed its way from the Houses of Parliament, through the streets of London to St Paul's Cathedral, we sat in awe at the sights and sounds that swirled around us.

The silent crowds filling the pavements were so close we could have touched them. We could see the anguish on their faces and the tears pouring down their cheeks. It was extraordinarily moving. We could hear the clip clop of the horses' hooves, the beating of the drums, the footsteps of the marching troops, the booming, nineteen-gun salute and the music of the massed bands, playing a medley of some of my grandfather's favourite tunes.

In the coffin's wake, once more carried on the shoulders of the bearer party, we processed up the steps of the cathedral in strict order of family seniority. The coffin was preceded by a group of honorary pall bearers, every one of whom had played a significant role in my grandfather's life, particularly during the war. They were all advanced in age, and valiantly climbed the steps without the aid of a handrail.

Frail and infirm though most of them were, only one had a real problem. Clement Attlee stumbled, bringing the procession to a brief halt. The bearers had rehearsed walking up the steps, but apparently not with a lead-lined coffin. As Attlee faltered, so did the bearers, causing the immense weight of the coffin to lurch backwards. It was a frightening moment; nevertheless, the guardsmen held firm and disaster was averted.

We followed the coffin up the aisle as the choir sang, 'I am the Resurrection and the Life.' We had been told that when we arrived at the nave, we need not make the traditional curtsey to the queen but could go directly to our seats. That was just as well, as the chaos of us all turning and curtseying might have descended into a farce, particularly if any of us had fallen over.

It was only one of the special concessions Her Majesty had made. The queen does not normally attend funerals and is always the last to arrive and the first to leave from any event. On this occasion she waived her precedence, not just to her former prime minister but also to his family. The royal family was seated facing the altar, with the Churchill family to the left. In the front row were Clementine, Randolph, Winston, Sarah, Mary, Christopher, Julian, Edwina, and me. Only Edwina and I are still alive.

After the service, which included some of my grandfather's favourite hymns: 'Onward Christian Soldiers', 'O God Our Help in Ages Past', 'Fight the Good Fight' and, acknowledging his American mother, 'The Battle Hymn of the Republic', we left the Cathedral in the order in which we had arrived.

The only difference was that Sarah, instead of getting back in the carriage with her mother and sister, left in a car with my grandfather's successor as prime minister, Sir Anthony Eden, who was too frail to continue to the burial. There had been concern by some members of the family that Sarah's heavy drinking might 'disrupt the service, spoil it for others, or prove to be an embarrassing distraction'. There was considerable pressure on her to be, 'too unwell' to attend her own father's funeral. Anthony Montague Browne, who had enjoyed a secret romance with Sarah, and I were determined that she should not be excluded. She had been devoted to her father, who called her, 'the Mule', and was probably his favourite child.

We knew we were up against strong opposition, but devised a plan that was finally agreed: Sarah would go into a nursing home for four days leading up to the funeral; Anthony would collect her on the morning of the day and take her to Westminster Hall. In addition, we conceded that she would not attend the private family burial at Bladon, next to Blenheim Palace, for fear that she would drink at lunch on the train journey. Sarah was not given a choice. It was the nursing home and the funeral or nothing. The fact that she left with Anthony Eden, who was extremely fragile, gave credence to the deception.

We left St Paul's, again by carriage, to ride to Tower Pier and then, on the launch, *Havengore*, along the Thames to Waterloo Station. Looking back as we left the cathedral, we saw that the entire royal family was standing on the steps to bid my grandfather a final farewell.

Once on board *Havengore*, as we were in the cabin below and the coffin was on the deck, we could see very little. But I could hear the mighty roar of the fly past overhead and see the cranes dipping their heads in salute, the only unscripted part of the day and, for me, one of the most moving. It is said that my grandfather had no hand in the funeral arrangements, apart from telling Anthony Montague Browne, 'Remember, I want lots of military bands at my funeral.' His wish was granted. There were nine.

When we reached Waterloo, the State Funeral was over, and Winston belonged to his family once more. We stood in silence while the coffin was lifted onto the train and placed in the luggage van. The Garter insignia was replaced by a single wreath of daffodils and lilies from the absent Sarah. The escort of the Grenadier Guards left, to be replaced by Grandpapa's old regiment, 4th Queen's Own Hussars, who stood guard for the final leg of the journey.

The aptly named locomotive, *Winston Churchill* moved off, hissing and belching smoke, to take my grandfather on his final journey back to where it had all started with his birth at Blenheim Palace, ninety years and so many adventures before. In the comfort of the Pullman car, we sat down to lunch washed down, of course, with Pol Roger. It was the first time we had felt able to relax since early morning.

Since Big Ben struck nine forty-five, I had felt that I was in a trance, swept along by a tide of events over which I had no control. This was one of the most orchestrated ceremonies ever held, but there was no sense that we were being directed. Everything just happened; or so it seemed to me.

It was incredible to see the railway lined with people for the entire journey from Waterloo to Long Hanborough, the nearest station to Bladon. We were all moved to tears. If Grandpapa had seen it, tears would also have been streaming down his face.

People were waving their handkerchiefs, saluting, or just watching silently from the station platforms. They stood in fields, on tractors; sat on ponies; children perched on their parents' shoulders; all witnesses to a sight that they would one day recount to their grandchildren with a lump in their throats. It seemed almost disrespectful to be eating while they mourned, but we had to fire ourselves up for the rest of the day.

The country road between the station and the village of Bladon was also lined with people. We followed on foot from the church gate to the graveside. After a short committal service, the coffin was lowered into the grave. The silence was broken by a metallic clatter and a gasp. A set of medals, clearly from the chest of one of the bearer party, was lying on top of the coffin. Professional as ever, they marched off smartly. We learned later that the medals were retrieved and returned to their owner.

Back in London, I found Sarah, completely sober and utterly wretched, waiting for me in the flat. We watched a re-run of the day's events on television. It was as though I was seeing it all for the first time. Earlier, it had almost been like taking part in a play, as if the action was somehow happening at some distance away from me. Now we were centre stage. I certainly had not, at the time, taken in the enormity of the day, but, as we watched on television, it began to sink in. It was extraordinary.

On 24 January 2015, half a century after Grandpapa's death, the whole family, about sixty of us, came together to celebrate his life. We had a service at Bladon, which included the hymns we had sung all those years before. It was a particularly sentimental occasion for the few of us who had been there on that day. For the younger members of the family, it was an opportunity to feel closer to the ancestor who, like their peers, they only knew in the pages of their history books.

A week later, on the fiftieth anniversary of the funeral we were back on *Havengore* retracing the journey from Tower Pier to Waterloo Station. Anthony Mather, the officer who had been in charge of the bearer party, and I were the only people present who had been on board on that January day in 1965.

Havengore is just a modest motor launch. It was merely carrying a few somewhat-less than famous people up the river. But the crowds were amazing. Hundreds of people lined the embankment and the bridges. Others stood watching and waving from the windows of their offices, some holding pictures of my grandfather. Few of those men and women would have been born when Winston Churchill died. No one on *Havengore* could have been of any interest to them, yet there they were; huge crowds to pay tribute to the greatest Briton of them all and the man I am proud to have called Grandpapa.

10

A Politician's Wife

In 1969, at the end of my marriage to Michael, I came back to London with Justin and embarked on life as a single mother. I exchanged my carefree existence in Kenya for a much more mundane and less affluent way of life. Although I was living in a very nice flat in Eaton Square, it was not a place of my own. It was my Aunt Sarah's, who had very kindly let me borrow it.

When I had told her that I was returning to London on my own she told me that she would lend me one of her two flats. I assumed that she meant the one in Earls Court, but this was not the case. Sarah had decided that, in my 'situation' Eaton Square would be much more suitable.

In Kenya, we had lived on Michael's expense account and therefore I knew nothing about paying bills. I hardly drank myself and had never had to concern myself with buying wine or stocking up with drink but now there was no one else to do it. I ordered what seemed appropriate from Andre Simon, the local wine merchant in Elizabeth Street: a case each of whisky, gin and vodka; six cases of red wine and six of white. With a single case perched precariously on his rusty bicycle, an exhausted delivery boy had to come innumerable times and pile up a mountain of alcohol in the hallway.

When he finally handed me the bill, I could not believe it. I had no idea what things cost, especially at London prices. I had to tell him that

I was sorry and that I would keep one bottle of whisky, vodka and gin and a case each of red and white wine. As for the rest, the poor boy had to take them all back on his rickety bicycle.

That summer Michael and I agreed that he would take Justin to Nairobi for the school holidays. I waved goodbye in floods of tears as he left with Nicky and his nanny, the Swedish baroness, who by then I was sure hoped to catch Michael's interest.

The deal was that he would return with Nicky at the end of the holidays but when I went to meet her at Heathrow in September she was on her own and told me, 'Daddy says you must go and collect Justin yourself'. It was a fairly obvious ploy. I do not think he expected me to change my mind but thought it worth a try. It was a futile gesture. I had no intention of staying.

By that time, I had rediscovered the boyfriend who had dumped me six years before just after my mother died. We ran into each other in Annabel's and I was surprised to discover that I found him just as attractive as I had before but although I had grown up, I was clearly still naïve. I went to collect Justin from Kenya on the understanding that we would get together on my return three days later. But that was not to be; he had gone off on holiday with a friend's au pair.

I had met Dennis Walters, the Conservative MP for Westbury in Wiltshire, on a visit a few months before and we were reintroduced shortly after my return. The timing was right. Dennis had just got divorced from his wife with whom he had a son and a daughter, and I was on my own. We had our new independence in common and, considering my strong Conservative pedigree on both sides of my family, I was apparently an ideal wife for a Tory politician. It certainly looked that way to everyone around us.

Like Michael, Dennis was an older man, this time the age difference was fourteen years. It might have been better if I had been interested in men of my own age but I had never had much in common with the younger ones and it was older men who came into my life at the critical moment and fate played its hand.

I decided I wanted my second wedding to be completely different from my first. In May 1970 Dennis and I were married at the British embassy in Paris where my uncle, Christopher Soames, was ambassador. I wore a brown and white midi dress which was fashionable at the time but with hindsight not very attractive! As the ceremony was about to begin my brother-in -law, with whom I had a tricky relationship, suddenly called a halt to the proceedings and insisted that we find out where my maternal great grandparents, Lord Randolph Churchill and Jennie Jerome had been married. Happily, we heard they were married in the same room, so the ceremony went ahead.

The day before our marriage an election was announced so our wedding photographs were taken at the same time as those for the election address, the flier that would be sent to every voter in the constituency.

We had the wedding lunch nearby at another Paris landmark, the Bristol Hotel followed by our wedding night at the Ritz. I will always remember looking up at the ceiling, which was ornately decorated with little putti, and thinking to myself, 'I hope these sweet cherubs bring me luck.' In my heart even at that moment I suspected I might have made a mistake. This was a thought I put to the back of my mind. We went to Rome for our honeymoon, complete with Clara, my Italian mother-in-law for company. I know this sounds very odd, but she was a wonderful woman, and one of the best things about the next ten years.

As a politician's wife, I was expected to open bazaars and garden parties and speak at coffee mornings. Public speaking was something I had always avoided even though my father always tried to persuade me to speak in in his constituency. At school, I remember being asked to read the lesson for a carol service and protesting defiantly that I would not do it. But when I was told that my grandfather would say I was a coward, I reluctantly agreed.

But as the new wife of the member of parliament I had to go and open the Christmas bazaar. I was really worried. I had only ever seen my mother do it, and in a very formal manner, so I assumed that was how it was done. Edwina confused me by asking me if I was going to make any jokes which unnerved me even more. I was a mature twenty-eight-year-old, there were no excuses to be made so off I went.

I took along my stepdaughter, Nicky Kennedy, who was staying with me. I had an awful premonition that something was going to go wrong, and Nicky was the trigger. The chairman of that particular constituency branch was a retired major general who I had seen in action during the election campaign. I knew, or I thought I knew exactly what he would say: congratulations on our wedding, my father would be mentioned; my grandfather and so on. However, before we got to the platform, when I had been introduced to the general, I had introduced him to 'my stepdaughter, Nicky Kennedy.' That had confused the old boy.

So, on my first appearance as Dennis's wife, when the general said, 'our member's wife needs no introduction. Without further ado I will ask Mrs Kennedy to declare the bazaar open.' There was a gasp from the audience. Although he quickly corrected himself, I was completely thrown. For me, his gaffe turned what was already a nightmare into a catastrophe.

When I got home, and Dennis asked how it had gone and I told him, how bad it was, he said, 'I suggest you don't speak anywhere outside the constituency.' His disheartening words rang in my head for years afterwards.

Before the election, and as part of our honeymoon, Dennis and I had visited seventy different places in the constituency, and I had to hear him make exactly the same campaigning speech seventy times. Dennis was happy about my Churchill connection as long as it did not make me seem more interesting than him. At one meeting I was introduced as, 'Our candidate's new wife' polite applause. Next 'Celia is the daughter of Duncan Sandys', who was very popular in the grassroots of the party, they all cheered, 'and the granddaughter of Winston Churchill', at which point they all stood up and cheered even more loudly. Dennis was not amused.

For public speaking, I then studied the way the constituency chairman's wife spoke and liked how she did it, no gracious lady airs just very relaxed and down to earth. I decided I was going to copy her, but I hated public speaking; and it still filled me with fear. I knew it was ridiculous but somehow it stayed with me for years. Now I love it and do it all the time.

Soon after we married Dennis and I bought a house in Tuscany which we both loved. We spent all the school holidays there. In 1971, our son Dominic was born at the Avenue Clinic in St John's Wood. I was married to Dennis for nearly ten years, twice as long as I was to Michael. But the relationship began to falter in the mid-70s, and we would part in 1979, when Justin was twelve and Dominic eight. I would then have seven years bringing them up on my own. I was going to have to have to learn how to live on my wits.

When we divorced, Dennis said, as if in warning, 'I'll see you living in Clapham', a dire threat to cast an ex-wife out into the sticks. He wanted me to suffer and, at that time, Clapham was thought to be a less than salubrious location. The irony is that it soon became a highly desirable place to live and it is now hard to find a family house for under a million pounds.

11

Living on my Wits

There were two elections in 1974, which made it a very busy year during which I had sensed that my relationship with Dennis was foundering. In 1975, Justin began prep school at Heatherdown near Ascot. Dominic was at day-school in London, so I had time on my hands and was beginning to feel at a loose end. More pointedly, the declining state of my marriage made it clear that, one day, I was going to need to look after myself and my boys.

Dennis's expertise as a pro-Arab specialist in Middle East affairs made up the lion's share of his political life. His many Arab contacts in London were very useful to me. I started to help people buy houses and met Desmond Corcoran, who owned the Lefevre Gallery in Bruton Street. I knew little about art, but I was well placed to introduce potential buyers to the gallery, mainly very rich Arabs. It was not a huge commitment, but if a sale resulted, I got a modest commission. It was yet another example of the old adage, 'It's not what you know, but who you know.'

Through another of Dennis's contacts, I started doing some work for a Lebanese builder. He asked me to work for him decorating the houses he was renovating for several rich Arabs in London and abroad. I do not think it mattered to him that I had no real experience. He liked the fact that I was the daughter of a cabinet minister and Churchill's granddaughter. I was happy to go along with this arrangement, as long as it was not abused.

I had few professional skills and little or no training for anything other than being a wife and mother. But I knew that, quite soon, I would need to be financially independent.

I discovered that I was quite good at decorating my own homes and making a profit from buyers who assumed that they were acquiring the lifestyle along with the fixtures and fittings. I found that doing up houses for someone else is completely different. You are interpreting taste that is not necessarily your own, but it was the offer on the table, so I accepted.

My first project was a big challenge mainly because I had to tackle it entirely on my own. It was for a medical centre in Harley Street and very different from anything I had done before, and I was way outside my comfort zone. I had to prepare the costs and source the materials with no clue how to set about it. Somehow, I muddled through and after that I insisted on having an assistant. I was lucky to find Jane Dawson, who had worked for a very good decorator and knew everything and everyone in the business. With her experience and expertise together, we could carry off the job.

I was told I could have a company car and could, within reason, name my make. So, I asked for a Triumph Stag, very fashionable at the time: it was a four-seater convertible coupe, a make that had featured in the Sean Connery Bond film, *Diamonds are Forever*. With its roof down and its throaty engine purring along London's sweltering streets during the memorably long-hot summer of 1976, my white Stag made me feel really good.

I played Demis Roussos on the in-car stereo system and took it on holiday to Italy, where it flew down the Autostrada way beyond the speed limit. My white Stag was the only car I ever fell in love with. I wish I still had it. My smart company car did not endear me to my colleagues: no one else in the office was given anything like it. They were very indignant and immediately demanded an upgrade which didn't endear me to the boss.

I met most of the owners of the houses I was asked to decorate and found some of them more challenging than others. One of them was Mahdi Al Tajir, the ambassador for the United Arab Emirates in

London, who was immensely rich and collected houses as others collect stamps. He had a house in Kent called Mereworth Castle, which is not a castle at all, but a beautiful early eighteenth century Palladian villa designed by Colen Campbell, the Scottish architect who pioneered the Georgian style.

I did not want to take on Mereworth as there were significant clashes of culture and taste to consider. When we drove up to the house, The ambassador said that he was going to put lamp posts along the drive. I had to find a polite way to tell him that lamp posts did not sit well with what the great Palladian architects had in mind nor indeed on the drive of an English country house.

Not wanting to be involved in destroying this rather wonderful house, I confined myself to the bathrooms. However, as everyone knows, usually from bad experience there are good plumbers and bad plumbers. Unfortunately, Mereworth attracted one of the latter type. One day, after someone had enjoyed a bath and pulled the plug, instead of draining away, the reverse happened. The entire contents of the sewage system began gurgling into the bath, which just goes to prove that even the vastly wealthy are not immune to the murky realities of waste disposal.

A little later, the ambassador asked me to change the decoration at his embassy in Princes Gate. He had tired of the silk on the walls of all his houses and wanted wallpaper. I took along several large books of wallpaper for him to look at and sat with him so that he could choose what he wanted. As I began, one of the books fell on the floor and opened on a random page, at which he said, 'Oh Celia, that's perfect! What good taste you have.' The die was cast for vibrant red walls. One of the diplomats told me it was like being back in the womb.

Another client was Sheikh Maktoum, the ruler of Dubai. Several female members of his entourage lived in a large building next to Harrods. My first visit was quite an experience: the women were cooking on little stoves on the floor. The central heating was turned up high and the rooms felt like saunas in a desert. The stifling heat had made all the doors warp and crack.

In another of his houses the gutters were all blocked. It transpired that the women had tossed their sanitary towels and tampons out of the windows into the gutters with disastrous results. We had to call in teams of specialists to clean up the place. I had many such trials to negotiate in this bizarre and unfamiliar world. I found that immensely and newly rich people often have their own uniquely eccentric qualities; they can behave very unpredictably; they are rarely satisfied, and they often do not want to pay!

One day I was sent to Dubai with a range of schemes for a number of grand projects. I cannot pretend that I prepared the details. Most of the leg work was done by Jane, but I was the front woman. The job was on a huge scale for several palaces and really difficult. Someone was going to make a lot of money out of it, but it was not going to be me.

I arrived with countless beautifully drawn plans, complete with samples and swatches of every kind. As a saleswoman, I was in my element. They looked at the entire proposal line-by-line and piece-by-piece and said, 'This is very interesting.' I did not see anything odd when they added, 'If you leave them here, you can come back tomorrow, and we'll give you our answer.'

Overnight, a member of the royal family died and the whole country closed down. I was stranded in Dubai for five days until they came out of mourning. Forty years ago, Dubai was completely different from how it is today and full of character and charm. Old buildings and dhows in the harbour; no palm-shaped island or artificial ski slope. Finally, I went back to see them. The man in charge said they liked everything and accepted the entire proposal. I was so relieved until he sent for some scissors. Every sample was cut in half. They kept one half and I was sent home with the other half.

I arrived back at the office in London and announced the deal. The owner's response was, 'Wonderful! We'll have a meeting tomorrow morning to go through everything.' He summoned the carpet supplier and said, 'Here's the carpet. I want one at half the price.' He did the same corner-cutting exercise for all the other materials. I knew this was not going to work and told him:

> You can do as you like, but you have to do it without me. I'm not going back to Dubai when the palaces are unveiled and watch them count how many fewer threads there are in their new carpets!

His reaction surprised me. 'You don't have to leave. Come and run the shop I'm buying in Mayfair.' I had always longed to run a shop. I was thrilled, so I said, 'Yes as long as I can decide what goes in it.' He said, 'Absolutely! Carte Blanche.'

My plan was to have a wonderfully stylish shop, combining good taste with the necessary flamboyance. I intended to have a tented room made into a coffee house where potential clients could come and relax. Dennis and I had a lot of Arab friends including all the ambassadors. I also met Mohamed Al Fayed around this time but did not have much to do with him, which with hindsight was rather fortunate. I do not believe we would have got on.

The shop was in a perfect spot on Mount Street, next door to Scott's Restaurant. I made some concessions to my clientele in the matter of ostentation, but the look was still as discreet and tasteful as I could manage. I was really pleased with the result and took a week off to go skiing and make plans for the opening. When I came back my beautiful shop had been completely transformed by an unseemly array of garish monstrosities! My boss had bought a dreadful collection of onyx and gilt, and just shoved it all in. That was the end of the dream. I moved on.

My grandmother, Clementine, died in 1977. She was my last tangible link to my grandfather. When he died in 1965, they had been married for more than fifty-six years, during which they had shared all the sadness and joy and success and failure of their extraordinary lives. Her role in being the rock from which he drew so much strength is well known, as is the strain which his dynamic temperament placed her under. Nevertheless, their love for one another was profound and enduring.

Following his death, she had been created a life peer as Baroness Spencer-Churchill, of Chartwell in the County of Kent and sat in the House of Lords as a crossbencher. Sadly, her growing deafness made it hard for her to make a major contribution to Parliament.

In the latter years of her life, inflation and rising expenses made it, in the opinion of her advisers, difficult for her to make ends meet. This in my opinion was ridiculous. There was not a bank in London that would not have jumped at the chance to lend to Churchill's widow. Embarrassingly old-age pensioners sent contributions, including teabags, to the nearly ninety-year-old who lived in a beautiful flat overlooking Hyde Park and employed a companion, a cook and a maid. In early 1977 she sent five of Grandpapa's paintings to auction. The sale went much better than expected and rescued her from her apparent financial difficulties. Only after her death was it discovered that she had destroyed the infamous Graham Sutherland portrait of Grandpapa that he had hated so much.

The painting had been commissioned by members of both Houses of Parliament to mark Churchill's eightieth birthday. When it was first unveiled, he said, with heavy irony, that it was, 'a remarkable example of modern art.'

Clementine had confided her distress at the portrait to Grace Hamblin, her devoted private secretary. Grace later became the curator of Chartwell when it passed to the National Trust and lived to the grand old age of 94 before her death in 2002. It was she who did made sure that the unflattering portrayal of my grandfather was never seen again.

The offending painting had been stored in a cellar at Chartwell, until, in the dead of night, Grace and her brother carried it into his van. They drove to his house several miles away and in the back garden, invisible from the street, built a bonfire, and committed the portrait to the flames. The next day she reported back to Clementine who said, 'We'll never tell anyone about this because after I go, I don't want anyone blaming you. But believe me, you did exactly as I would have wanted.'

The real story of what Sutherland called, 'an act of vandalism' only emerged quite recently when a forgotten tape recording of a conversation with Grace was discovered in the Churchill Archive at Churchill College Cambridge.

My grandmother suffered a heart attack and died at her London home on 12 December 1977. She was 92 years old and had outlived her husband by almost thirteen years, as well as three of her five children. She was buried with them and her husband at Bladon.

A service of Thanksgiving was held in Westminster Abbey on 24 January 1978, the thirteenth anniversary of the death of her husband. The prime minister, Jim Callaghan and Margaret Thatcher, leader of the opposition came with members of the royal family and representatives of over sixty countries. The Abbey was packed.

It was a very moving day, full of sadness, of course, but also uplifting as we reflected on such a wonderful life. My cousin, Winston, read an extract from the sermon preached almost seventy years before by Dr James Welldon, who had been Winston's headmaster at Harrow, in St

Margaret's Westminster, at the wedding of a young, newly-appointed cabinet minister, Mr Winston Churchill, and Miss Clementine Hozier, 'May your lives prove a blessing, each to the other and both to the world, and may you pass in the Divine mercy from strength to strength and from joy to joy.' Dr Welldon, affectionately known as 'Porker' by the boys at Harrow, was clearly a man of some insight.

My grandmother's death also led to another 'happening' in my life, a rather scary one! She had left all her granddaughters a piece of jewellery. So, I got ready to go and collect mine on my way out to dinner. I took off my own jewellery, put it on the bed and got into the bath in our flat in Warwick Square. The door to the bedroom was open slightly and, as I lay there soaking, I saw a shape walk past the door wearing a fur coat that looked very much like my red fox. Then I saw a second which bore an uncanny resemblance to my racoon coat.

I shouted, 'Who's there?' at which the door was pulled shut with a bang. Fortunately, there was a key in the door, so I jumped out of the bath, splashing water everywhere, and locked it. There was a telephone in the bathroom, and I was able to call the secretary in Dennis' office downstairs, who called the police.

The police were very nice, but there was little they could do. The thieves were long gone, and nothing was ever found. They had taken my favourite jewellery, the pieces I wore every day as well as the fur coats. The next morning, feeling somewhat sorry for myself and thankful that I had had a lucky escape, I took myself off to Harrods, where my father was a director and therefore entitled to a big discount.

I had by chance been to Harrods the day before and tried on a beautiful mink, which I thought I could only dream about. Now it was a different matter. I claimed on the insurance and took it home.

When my father discovered my extravagance, he was horrified, suggesting, disparagingly, that a 'cloth coat from Jaeger would have been much more suitable for someone of my station in life.' I didn't really want to know what that was because I was sure I would not like it, so I didn't enquire.

12

Gorgeous Gianni

By 1978, my marriage to Dennis was well and truly over. I do not believe in soldiering on when there is clearly no hope for the future, either it is right, or it is not. I believe that there is little point persevering with something that is a lost cause, because eventually you end up as complete enemies. But I had a big problem, Dennis would not accept that we had no future.

In the summer, we went as usual to La Capellina, the lovely house we had bought eight years before, near Lucca in Tuscany. In desperation, I decided that I needed to arrange a 'flirtation' to act as a beacon to make Dennis accept the reality of the state of our marriage. I found a nice Italian who was more than happy to go around with me and to create the strong impression that I was having an affair. Italians love a bit of intrigue. He knew I was using him as a decoy, but found it quite amusing and in any case, we had a good time together. Anyway, the ruse worked, and Dennis finally accepted the situation.

That Christmas, the boys and I went skiing and Dennis said he would come and see us. It was very awkward, especially when I fell and broke my hand, an injury which still plagues me to this day, and my estranged husband had to help me with mundane tasks like fastening and unfastening my bra!

The following year, 1979, became a significant year in my life. The country reached an important turning point in its history and so did I in my life's journey.

In March, the IRA escalated its already menacing terrorist campaign when the MP, Airey Neave, was blown up in his car as he drove out of the car park of the Palace of Westminster. The day before, the date for the general election in May had been announced and Neave was chosen as the terrorists' victim. They believed that, should the Conservatives win the election, which seemed highly likely, he was almost certain to become the new secretary of state for Northern Ireland and would have a major impact in the province.

Neave was very close to the Conservative leader Margaret Thatcher and his death was intended as a bloody message to her about what she should expect from them as prime minister. The message was heeded, but perhaps not in the way the IRA intended and went a long way towards hardening her position about the IRA. I remember the day well, especially when I realised that Dennis was not far away when the bomb went off.

There was little doubt that the Conservatives were going to win the election. They had a huge lead in the opinion polls and Jim Callaghan's Labour government had had a disastrous few months. We had endured the 'winter of discontent', which saw Britain crippled by industrial strife and the economy suffering from severe unemployment and high inflation.

It did not help the national mood that the winter was particularly harsh, causing much chaos and a significant economic downturn. The newspapers were full of images of mountains of rubbish piled high in the streets and, because of unofficial strikes by gravediggers in some parts of the country, lurid stories of the dead lying unburied in emergency mortuaries. Somewhat naively, when asked about the crisis, Callaghan view was summarised succinctly as, 'Crisis? What Crisis?' The press had a field day and in a single famous headline he had sealed his fate and that of his party.

With my marriage to Dennis in its death throes, I went looking for a little adventure. By chance, I met the next man in my life: a very attractive and charming Italian called, Gianni Clerici. He was handsome, elegant, and great fun. Perhaps not a future husband, but, as a Latin lover, ideal!

The meeting, as is often the case, occurred unexpectedly. I was in Milan and had asked a friend if she knew anyone who could make me a silk shirt. Indeed, she did, 'Go and see my friend Gianni, he makes the best shirts in Milan.' That was Gianni. He looked just like the actor, Alain Delon, the French heartthrob of the 1960s; I was smitten.

Of course, although he was ten years older than me and by then I was thirty-six, like all Italians, he had a mother of some significance in his life, with whom he still lived. Never underestimate an Italian mother! We spent a few days together and got on very well. When I got back to London, where Dennis and I still shared a flat in Pimlico, a bunch of flowers arrived that was so enormous it was impossible to get it through the front door. I did not try to explain it to Dennis!

Although our marriage was over, I had to campaign with Dennis for the election. He had had the family photograph done for his campaign literature. He needed me to be there; I had no choice. But it was not a happy time. Just before Election Day he said, 'I think you should go away. Why don't you go and stay with Edwina in New York?' I suppose he thought I might embarrass him in some way.

I was thrilled to go because Gianni was about to go to New York so for me, it was perfect timing. I went to join him. Though ostensibly I was with Edwina, in fact, Gianni and I had a wonderful time staying at the Pierre on 5th Avenue.

When it came to election night, you could ring the British embassy in Washington for a progress report. The Embassy staff must have thought something of great significance was happening in Westbury because of the number of calls I made. Dennis won with a majority of almost 14,000.

Margaret Thatcher won a majority in parliament with the biggest swing in votes since Clement Attlee's landslide victory over my grandfather in 1945. As time went on, we soon began to realise that the country's first female prime minister was going to be very different and that she would create a very different Britain.

The last time I went to the constituency from London, Dennis had asked his secretary to give me a parcel for him. Only when I took it out of the car did I realise it was a case of champagne for him to share with his new girlfriend. I really did not care but it was not an elegant way to behave. I had already discovered what one could call 'foreign bodies' in the fridge, things neither Dennis nor I would ever eat; an all too obvious indication of another 'presence' in the house and not an ethereal one!

It was a surreal time. I had disappeared from Westbury like a nun going over the wall. I was there one day, in the centre of all activities, then gone. Sadly, there is always a pile of debris in the aftermath of changing circumstances. I could not say goodbye or say thank you to all the people who had befriended me. I had gone and did not exist anymore. I did subsequently make contact with some of them, whom I still see occasionally.

Even though Dennis and I divorced at the end of 1979, we still shared the house in Tuscany for a while. So, in the summer of 1980 we shared it between us. I had Gianni there for a while and Dennis had his girlfriend there. All very civilised, or not, depending on one's point of view. Dennis went on to marry the champagne drinker, Bridgett Shearer, in 1981. They divorced ten years later.

To start with Gianni and I spoke French to one another. His English was a very crude version picked up from his Japanese customers and I had acquired only 'horticultural' Italian from our Tuscan gardener. My French was good enough from my schooldays in Paris and Gianni was in the fashion business in which the lingua franca is French.

Everyone loved Gianni. He was so much fun. We went to Scotland to stay with George and Philippa Jellicoe and while we were there, he decided to buy a kilt and all the kit that goes with it. He looked great but there were of course no occasions for him to wear it. Every so often he would disappear from the dinner table and return all dressed up to the sound of Scottish music. One day we went to Turnbull and Asser and he spotted my grandfather's siren suit in the showcase, so he ordered one of his own. He was a showman. He was friends with the Giorgio Armani set, but never made it to the top himself.

Not only did Gianni have an Italian mother, but when I met him, he also had an Italian lover, an older woman, Romilda, who was the wife of a very well-known man from Turin. He was the owner of a major drinks company, who, apparently, knew all about Gianni and seemed to accept it. She was a fair bit older than him and obviously besotted with him. To my horror, when he told her about me, she invited us both to stay with her and her husband. What a prospect!

It was my birthday, but it was to prove to be the least enjoyable celebration in my life. Romilda and her husband had a huge house behind large, ornate gates, which, with an ominous clang, closed behind us when we arrived, evoking an overwhelming sense of foreboding. The husband was charming; perhaps I should have run off with him, but she was obviously playing some sort of diabolical game. I have no idea why we agreed to it, but Gianni was put in a room at the family end of the house, and I was assigned one in a distant wing, far away from everybody else.

We went out to a party, where Italian tongues wagged the entire evening with me clearly the subject of the conversations. When I went to bed that night, I felt sure that the lady of the house had a grisly plan for my disposal, so I jammed a chair under the door handle and spent a sleepless night in fear of impending doom.

The next morning, thankful still to be in one piece, I told Gianni that we were leaving, and without delay. So we did, but as we got into the car, Romilda jumped in the back! We drove all the way to Milan, a two-hour drive, with her threatening to jump out all the way. It was high drama and nerve-racking.

I booked into a hotel and Gianni took Romilda, back to his mother in an attempt to resolve the crisis. Apparently, at some stage that night the Milanese Croce Verde, a sort of Italian St John's Ambulance, was called, to calm her down. After a huge drama she returned to Turin to her charming husband and her clanging gates.

Like most Italians, Gianni was a great traveller. One day we went to New York from where we were going to join some Italian friends of his in Mexico City for a week's holiday. But they changed their plans and decided they were going to Acapulco. Of course, Acapulco on the warm west coast, has quite a different climate from the altitude of Mexico City. Again, we were staying at The Pierre overlooking Central Park, and, before I knew about the change of plans, I had bought a lovely new winter wardrobe. I was not going to take that to Acapulco, so I left it with the hotel concierge to await my return.

The temperature in Acapulco is almost always in the high eighties Fahrenheit ($\pm$ 30° C) and very much a beach, sun and surf resort, whereas Mexico City is at least twenty degrees cooler. So, all I had to wear in Acapulco was a silk pyjama suit that Gianni had given me. As soon as we arrived, we went to a street market and I bought myself a bikini and a shirt. It turned out we were going to have lunch and dinner with the same group of twelve Italians every day. Oh dear!

They were terribly elegant and sophisticated and deeply shocked by my limited attire: my clothes from the street market and one pyjama suit every night. I did not mind their disapproval nearly as much as I hated the midnight dinners and the humid weather. It was for me a nightmare holiday and I will always be remembered as that very shabbily dressed English woman!

When we got back to The Pierre, my clothes had vanished without a trace. I had not even worn them. I was able to recover the cost on the insurance, but it would have been nice to have had at least one wearing of each of them.

My stay at the Pierre also had another Italian link. An Italian friend of mine called me and we had a bizarre conversation, which illustrates how perverse people can be, especially very rich people, for she was very rich. I had mentioned that I was going to New York with Gianni and would be staying at the Pierre. She was very excited and asked me to do her a favour. She said, 'I have managed to collect almost all their silver collection, but I'm one piece short. Could you get me a soup tureen?' She expected me to leave the hotel with a large silver soup tureen secreted about my person! Needless to say, I left the rather unattractive hotel silver collection intact.

Gianni and I spent two wonderful years together. We never discussed the future, probably because I think we knew we did not have one. I moved between Milan and London in the term time. During the school holidays we went skiing or to the house in Tuscany.

During the first summer, we took Justin to Cap Ferrat in the South of France. When Gianni returned to Milan Romilda told him she knew exactly where we had been and even repeated our conversations in restaurants. It turned out that she had sent her bodyguard to follow us and report back.

This was alarming but not the end of her nefarious activities. When I got back to the Capellina there was a threatening letter waiting for me. The ominous note told me that I should be afraid for my family and that bad things might happen. I showed it to Dennis, who was going to be there with Justin and Dominic for two weeks while I went away with Gianni. He called in the police who gave him a gun and agreed to patrol and watch the house in case of trouble.

On my return, I found that when he left, Dennis had dismissed the police and returned the gun, even though he was clearly not the target of the menacing message. In any case, the threat was probably only meant to scare me and discourage Gianni.

We went to America several times on one occasion to sell Gianni's shirts at a garment fair in Dallas. I have always liked selling and enjoyed it very much.

Gianni, Justin, and I had a fabulous holiday with George and Philippa Jellicoe at their warm and chaotically wonderful holiday home in the extreme north of Scotland. Justin was good friends with their children, so everyone was happy. Gianni loved it and they liked him.

It is said that all good things come to an end and so it was with Gianni and me. We went to Ken Lo's restaurant, *Memories of China*, in Ebury Street and he asked me to marry him. He was not someone to marry; he was someone to have fun with. Sadly, he had decided he was ready for marriage, but I was not. That brought an end to my Italian idyll.

Later, when I saw my stepmother, she said, 'You look a bit sad.' I replied, 'Yes, Gianni and I have split up.' She looked startled, 'Gianni asked me to marry him.' She looked even more surprised, 'Why don't you?' When I told her that it would not have lasted, she surprised me by saying, 'Well, you could always divorce him.' to which I said, 'Perhaps, but I'd rather not go into marriage planning a divorce.'

I did see Gianni occasionally after that. He gave me a gold bracelet instead of the diamond ring he had planned which was quite elegant of him and then had an affair with a good friend of mine. But he and I stayed friends. Later on, he married a very nice rich widow, which suited him perfectly.

In the winter of 1980, Justin, Dominic, and I went skiing with the Jellicoes and several of their children. George was an exceptional character. A politician of forthright opinions, a very brave man typical of those who had performed extraordinary deeds in the Second World War. He was one of the first members of the SAS and went on to set up the Special Boat Squadron in Greece. He was also a brilliant and fearless skier especially after a good lunch. A prodigious skier. George and Philippa, who I liked a lot, had children about the same age as Justin and Dominic.

One day, the children were teasing me about my skiing, so to put them in their place, our guide, Pierre Gruneberg, the most famous ski-guide in Courchevel suggested we ski the Grand Couloir a famous precipitous black run. I had skied it several times before but always when the snow was soft so did not regard it as fraught with danger.

As we reached the point of no return, we noticed that there was a very ominous stretch of ice right across our descent, but we went down anyway. I did not even think about the ice, as I was concentrating on the boys in front of me. But when we reached the patch of ice, I slipped and went hurtling down the hill on my back. Pierre saw me and dived forward to grab my legs and we both hurtled down the mountain, he on his face and I on my back.

We were going extremely fast. Pierre could not hold onto me. I was on my own. As I looked up at the beautiful blue sky, I knew I would die from a broken neck. I had had a row with George Jellicoe the night before and I thought that I would never be able to make my peace with him. Much worse, I worried about the impact on my boys when they discovered my shattered body, bloodied and broken.

Eventually, after a terrifying fall with my neck crashing on the hard ice the slope evened out and I came to a stop. I just lay there looking up at the blue cloudless sky until I realised, I was not dead. I managed to get up and saw Pierre and the boys up on the mountain, collecting the debris of my fall: skis, sticks, sunglasses, hat all of which I had somehow shed as I careered down the mountain. Poor Pierre's face was skinned raw. He was a dreadful sight, but I seemed fine. I skied the next day, if a little gingerly, but felt alright. Then, a week later, I was in the cinema and, suddenly, could not hold my head up.

I had an x-ray, only to discover that I had indeed chipped the seventh bone in my neck, what my mother used to call the Dowager's Hump. I was put in a collar and recovered but suffered headaches for years afterwards. I eventually went to 'Bob the Healer', a former policeman, recommended by my friend Kristina who I had worked with at the General Trading Company. I do not know what he did, but he cured me. It seemed like mumbo jumbo, but it worked for me. It also worked for the actor, Robert Hardy, who swore that Bob had cured his cancer but sadly not for my brother Julian. Whatever he did seemed like a miracle. I had been plagued by my neck for more than ten years and I have not had a problem since.

13

More Adventures

When Dennis and I parted we divided our flat in Warwick Square. This was not an ideal arrangement and I soon moved to a temporary flat on Albert Bridge Road in Battersea. Then I bought a really glamorous house in Bloomfield Terrace in Pimlico, which belonged to my cousin, Charles Churchill, and his wife Jane. It was a lovely house more suited to parties than family life.

One evening I was at a dinner party and was sitting next to the famous publisher, George Weidenfeld, who asked me where I lived. I said, 'Bloomfield Terrace,' to which he replied rather patronisingly:

Quite sweet pretty little houses in Bloomfield Terrace. But if you ever get the chance, there's one where you should put your nose round the door, because it's really special. It is like a country house with a lovely hall which takes you down the stairs to an amazing, perfect cube room.

When everyone was leaving, I said:

Do come and see me I live in one of those sweet pretty little houses. but I think you know mine, when you go in there's a lovely hall and stairs leading to a perfect cube room.

It was a wonderful house for me, but the boys lived crammed into the basement. I was able to hire it out to film companies for shoots, which brought in a bit of money and was also fun. I had a good friend in London at the time, Bill Tuohy, the UK correspondent for the *Los Angeles Times* and a Pulitzer prize winner for his reporting of the Vietnam War. We both knew lots of people and whenever life got dull one of us would give big party to cheer things up.

I carried on trying to make enough money to pay the bills. One day I got a call from someone I had met in New York who worked in PR. She asked me if I was free because she wanted to send someone to London, who had never been to the city before. He was the head of the New York Futures Exchange and wanted to meet everyone in the City. Would I help?

I agreed of course, but my immediate concern was to find out what a future was. I then called an old boyfriend of mine, who was the chairman of one of the big banks in London. It was more than twenty years since I had spoken to him, but he was the only person I knew who could help. He was very nice and said:, 'It's more than my marriage is worth for me to help you, but I'll give you my PA for the duration of the visit and he will deal with it all for you.'

We had dinner parties at my house and in the private dining room in Annabel's. He got all the introductions he needed in the City and the whole trip was a great success. I got well-paid of course and all the expenses were taken care of, but then I made a big mistake. After it was over, the New York PR company asked for a full report of everything we had done and who we had met. Naively, I passed on every detail. By doing this I ensured that they then had all the contacts they needed and would no longer need my services in the future.

1981 was a good year for making friends and I met three people who remain close to this day: Adrien Ellul, Linda Duncan and Gilli Newson.

In the summer of 1981, Justin went to stay with his godmother, my friend Mary Oppenheimer, who had arranged a safari to Botswana. There was a spare place and she persuaded me to go as well. What I did not know was that the spare place was in the same tent as a very famous and attractive man, who must remain anonymous. She was matchmaking. I was there with Justin and he was there with his children.

At one of the camps the manager told us that we must not leave the tent at night and that, if we needed to, we could use a pot next to the bed to answer a call of nature. I was obviously far too embarrassed to use the pot with this glamorous man in the tent, so in the middle of the night, I ignored the warning, and went to the loo block. Half an hour later, all hell broke loose. Right outside our tent five lions were devouring a buffalo. The next morning, I was horrified to see the ground by the tent flap was covered with the paw prints of lions. Two years later, the cook in the same camp was eaten by a lion.

I had had a very close shave! As for the matchmaking, it was fun while it lasted but that was all. Botswana is a wonderfully romantic place.

I then helped my sister Edwina with an art exhibition of my grandfather's paintings. I handled the London end, then we sailed with the paintings on the QE2 to New York. As I had a friend who had a fireworks company, I asked him if he would like to do the fireworks in Central Park for the opening of the exhibition and he agreed. What I had not anticipated was that the Mafia had a grip on the licensing of fireworks in the city and soon put a stop to our plans. So, no fireworks; I am not averse to a challenge but was not prepared to take on the Mafia in their own backyard.

While I was with Gianni, I met an Italian exile living in Switzerland, Victor Emanuel, the son of the former king of Italy, a somewhat dubious character, totally lacking in charm. He had the grand title, the duke of Savoy, and, had the Italian monarchy not been abolished in 1946, would have been heir to the throne. One day I got a call from a mutual friend asking if I knew anyone at the civil and military aircraft manufacturer, British Aerospace, which I did. She was delighted, because, she said, 'Victor Emanuel would like to meet them.' My wheeler-dealing was about to begin in earnest.

Alec Sanson was fairly high up in BAE and someone I knew from when I was married to Dennis. When I explained what I wanted, he said, 'I'll be there in five minutes.' When he arrived, he said, 'I have been trying to meet him for ten years.' I realised I was on to a good thing.

I made the introduction and set up a meeting with Victor Emanuel, who was working with an Argentinian admiral who was coming to Europe to buy military hardware. Once I had done the introduction and set up the meeting, I would have been out of it, but would receive a fee for the introduction.

The meeting was scheduled for Friday 2 April 1982. I remember the date clearly because it became a date of some significance in our history. The evening before, we got a telex saying that the admiral was, 'unavoidably delayed'. It was soon obvious why. Friday 2 April was the day an Argentinian task force invaded the Falkland Islands in the South Atlantic, the beginning of a seventy-four-day conflict which cost the lives of over nine hundred British and Argentinian servicemen.

The deal was lost and, with it, a nice commission that would have come my way. On the other hand, it would have been very distressing if the deal had gone through a little earlier and I had been involved in weapons used by our enemies against our own forces.

Around that time, I was introduced to an extraordinary half-Lebanese, half-Danish man who owned the Caviar House in Zurich and Geneva Airports and wanted to open one at Heathrow but had completely failed to make the right contacts. He said he would give me £55,000 if I could get him into Heathrow. I did not know anything about caviar, or Heathrow, but I thought I would give it a try; £55,000 was a lot of money. I would have done it for £5,000!

My network worked for me yet again. I only had to make one call to an acquaintance of mine, who said he knew the man in charge at Heathrow. The meeting was arranged, I made the introduction, and I had a letter agreeing to the £55,000 fee. George, whose surname I have forgotten, came around, chased me around the coffee table and brought me a present of the most wonderful royal caviar. The obvious thing to do was to share it with Eddie, the person who had made the introduction. So I invited him round, but George was furious! I could not understand why as he surely would not have wanted to eat his own caviar.

A few months later, I got a letter saying, 'you've been unsuccessful in bringing off this deal, so our letter of agreement is null and void.' Two days later, I met Eddie, who said, 'Isn't it great that George got the contract at Heathrow.' I could not believe it. He had cut me out of the deal that I had set up!

I went to see George who had his daughter with him and told him, 'I can't believe anyone could behave in such an ungentlemanly fashion.'

He was outraged and said, 'I can't believe you can talk to me like that in front of my daughter.' It was an impasse, but I decided not to take the legal route, which appeared too expensive and too risky, and settled for £17,000, which would have been quite a good fee in the first place.

I was never able to go past the Caviar House while that awful man still owned it without wanting to throw something at it. It taught me a sad lesson do not assume you can trust anyone where money is involved.

Just before Christmas, 1983. Justin, Dominic, and I were preparing to go to South Africa to stay with my friend, Mary Oppenheimer. The day before we were leaving, I had an appointment to go to my hairdresser on Sloane Street and Justin, who was sixteen at the time, went to Harrods to do some Christmas shopping.

When I came out of the hairdresser, I was met by an eerie silence, so unusual in the middle of London. The IRA had exploded a car bomb outside Harrods. I was horrified that Justin may have been caught up in it. I rang home, there was no answer; there were no mobile phones in those days. So I went to Harrods and of course it was impossible to get anywhere near it. I went home; there was no-one there. I had to wait in agony for several hours before discovering that he had indeed gone to Harrods but had walked in one side (very near where the bomb went off) and out the other and gone for a walk in Hyde Park.

It was a real tragedy. There had been very little warning and three police officers, and three members of the public were killed. The next morning, we decided to do some shopping at Harrods on the way to the airport. It was deserted, but the staff were so pleased to see us, we were greeted with, 'thank you for shopping at Harrods', and given a present at every counter.

1984 was not a particularly good year and it passed rather uneventfully. I had an alcoholic boyfriend who I thought I could sort out, but it was, as everyone told me, impossible. I would get him sober for a while, then he would go on long drunken binges which were horrible and inevitably we split up. After my experience with my aunt Sarah, I should have realised it was impossible.

In 1985, I met a Pakistani businessman called Moodi Farouki, who was the agent for British Aerospace, in Pakistan. He feared he was going to lose the agency and asked me if I would help him. Alec Sansom was still at British Aerospace, so I rang him and asked him what I should do. He arranged a meeting and when I arrived, I was met by the man in charge of the Middle East, India and Pakistan who introduced himself as Ken Perkins.

Ken organised a meeting with Farouki, who was sophisticated or diplomatic but rather endearing. I had never been to that sort of meeting before and Moodi's future was in my hands. Fortunately, the meeting went well, and I persuaded the British Aerospace team that Moodi and I would go to Pakistan with them to assess how he and his operation were working. Moodi made it through the inquisition. Not only that, he had a big deal in the pipeline with the Pakistani military for missiles for their warships.

In April 1986, the deal was announced in parliament by Margaret Thatcher and in Pakistan by the President, Zia ul Haq and the contract was on their desks waiting for signature. Then everything changed. Zia's political opponent, Benazir Bhutto, who had been in exile in Britain, went back to Pakistan and President Reagan sanctioned a US bombing raid on Libya.

The political climate across the whole of the Muslim world changed and the whole deal collapsed. It would have been a major deal, so it was fortuitous that I had not committed the money before I had it in my bank account. The experience made me realise how quickly everything can vanish. Even so, although I had no professional qualifications and few relevant skills, I began to realise how possible it was for a 'woman with contacts' and the know-how to use them, to make a living for herself. I suppose it was ever thus.

I knew the Clark brothers of Plessey, John and Michael, whose family was the driving force behind the company. Plessey had grown from a modest galvanising company based in Ilford, to become, by the 1980s, the UK's leading telecommunications company. Thanks to John and Michael, I found myself with a group of Indians flying around in helicopters to meet the Clarks and visit their various manufacturing bases all over the country.

I cannot even remember what the potential deals were, but I know nothing ever came of them. Nevertheless, it was great fun amidst interesting times, not only that, travelling to Pakistan with Ken Perkins and his team opened a completely new in my life.

14

A Merciful Death

My Aunt Sarah was multi-talented: a fine actress; an accomplished writer; she could sing and paint; and wrote lovely poetry. As a young dance student, she fantasised about becoming Fred Astaire's favourite partner. Seeing the poster of her hero on her bedroom wall, my grandfather poured cold water on his daughter's dream, 'Hmm,' he said. 'Facts are better than dreams.' Seventeen years later, Sarah did dance with Fred Astaire, in the film, *Wedding Bells*.

She starred in the stage version of the classic thriller, *Gaslight,* and made the cover of *Life* magazine. Her career included the theatre in both Britain and the United States; several films: dramas, comedies, and musicals; and roles in television, including the Scotland Yard police drama, *Fabian of the Yard*.

During the war, Sarah worked in photographic reconnaissance in the Women's Auxiliary Air Force, which played a very important role in the war effort. In fact, the WAAFs were crucial during the Battle of Britain in areas like meteorology, radar, aircraft plotting and in telephonic and telegraphic communications. In her book, *Evidence in Camera,* fellow reconnaissance specialist, Constance Babington Smith, records that Sarah worked closely on the interpretation of photographs for the 1942 invasion of North Africa, *Operation Torch*. Known by her married name, Sarah Oliver, Babington Smith says she was 'a quick and versatile interpreter.'

Later, long before I was lucky enough to travel with him, she became my grandfather's travelling companion. She was alongside him at the Teheran and Yalta Conferences of 1943 and 1945, respectively.

Despite her intense and sometimes volatile artistic temperament, she was my grandfather's favourite and struck all of us as the most enchanting and vivacious person. She was like a fairy godmother. Although she married three times, she had no children of her own and would dote on Edwina and me. She would appear with the most exciting, if sometimes unsuitable presents, diaphanous nightdresses when I was far too young, or bedside lights in the shape of cherubs. She gave me my first tights, which she had brought from America.

She was a generous and warm-hearted person who charmed everyone. When my marriage to Michael ended and I came back to London, she lent me one of her flats, not the modest one in Earls Court, but the much nicer one in Eaton Square. She felt that Earls Court was not suitable for someone in my 'situation' so she moved in there, letting me live in her 'good address', which would be a springboard to my new life once my divorce came through.

Her first husband was Vic Oliver, the actor and comedian, who was a lot older than her. They married in 1936, when she was twenty-two and he was thirty-eight. I suspect he must have been very appealing to an aspiring young thespian like Sarah.

Born in Vienna, the son of an Austrian baron, he was a fine athlete and became Austrian junior tennis champion in 1914, before serving in the Austrian cavalry in the First World War. He then worked in banking and manufacturing before he gave up a medical degree at the University of Vienna to pursue his love of music. He played the violin and studied under Gustav Mahler, before going to America as a conductor.

While working in America, he discovered his gift for comedy by chance, when he had to apologise to his audience for a mishap during a performance. A new career as a comedian took him all over the United States and then to London where he became very well known for his deferential, modest humour and for deliberately playing the violin badly. He was I believe great fun to be with but probably less fun as a husband.

Sarah met him when they played together in a C. B. Cochran revue and they became secretly engaged. My grandfather never approved of their wedding. There is an anecdote, probably apocryphal, that at a dinner party at which Oliver was present, my grandfather was asked whom he most admired. He replied, 'Mussolini.' When asked why, he replied, 'Because he had the good sense to shoot his son-in-law!' If true, I am sure Oliver's own sense of comedy meant that he took the barb with an appropriate pinch of salt.

Unfortunately, the marriage did not survive the war and they were divorced in 1945, by which time Oliver had become a very popular radio entertainer. His Jewish background and his fame were enough for him to be put on Hitler's notorious 'Blacklist' of those to be killed immediately after the invasion of Britain. He was also Roy Plomley's very first guest on *Desert Island Discs* in January 1942.

I cannot be sure at what point alcohol began to be a problem in Sarah's life. Perhaps she had started drinking seriously when she was married to Vic and was living in a world where heavy drinking was commonplace. But I have always believed that Sarah's rapid decline into the clutches of alcohol began when she was with her second husband, Anthony Beauchamp, He was a society photographer, the son of the artist, Ernest Entwistle and his wife, portrait photographer, Vivienne Mellish.

They married in 1949. He was clearly not a very nice man. I must have been about five when they came stay with us in Hampshire. Anthony gave me a piggyback and dropped me in the middle of a bramble bush. I was wearing little shorts. I never liked him after that. He was often quite nasty to Sarah and killed himself with an overdose of barbiturates in 1957.

When Sarah was younger, my mother had felt protective of her younger sister and this carried on into adulthood. When she died and Edwina left for New York, that responsibility fell to me.

She once described herself as, 'the lamb who strayed from the fold' and that she, 'burned her scandals at both ends'. For all her magical qualities, she was a walking disaster whenever she drank too much. Her addiction to the bottle eventually took its toll. I have early memories of my mother bailing her out from Gerald Road police station. She was often picked up for making a nuisance of herself on the street, and once remanded in Holloway Prison.

There were times, like at the Dorchester reception for my wedding to Michael, when I could not step in to save her from herself, when her unfortunate intervention on behalf of my mother led to a furious dressing down from my Aunt Mary on an island in the middle of Park Lane.

Sarah married her third husband, Henry, the twenty-third Lord Audley, in 1962. He was undoubtedly the love of her life and the only husband of whom her parents approved. He was descended from an ancestor ennobled in 1313 in the reign of Edward II. They were living happily in Marbella, which at that time was still unspoiled, when he suffered a heart attack and died. He was only forty-nine years old and they had been married for just a year. It was a terrible blow for Sarah, who had woken up to find her husband dead next to her and quickly went into decline in a spiral of drinking.

My grandmother gave my mother ten thousand pounds and asked her to go to Spain and make the funeral arrangements. When she got there, she found that Henry's body had been removed and impounded and would only be released on payment of twice the amount that my grandmother had provided. The unspoken threat was that details of Sarah's pub crawl would be leaked to the press. There being no acceptable alternative the payment was made, and the funeral took place. Sarah, who had got married in my Ascot clothes, buried her husband in my only black suit. She went to live in Rome for a while before eventually returning to her Eaton Square flat.

While I was living on my own with my small son Justin, she would call me when I was needed. I remember a particular SOS early one morning. Sarah had fallen and hurt herself. I jumped out of bed and arrived to find an ambulance at the door, about to take her to Westminster Hospital.

I went in the ambulance with her. She looked a real mess. It became apparent that the accident had happened the previous night, but she and her boyfriend of the moment were either too drunk to realise she needed medical attention or had decided they did not want to call an ambulance until she had sobered up.

By the time we got to the emergency department, Sarah was rather high on gas and air, and looking very ragged. The doctor came and diagnosed a broken hip and said they would have to operate. I asked when this would be, and he replied, 'probably within 48 hours', 'but she's in pain. Can't it be done sooner?' 'It doesn't work like that. There's a queue', he said firmly, 'This is the National Health Service you know.' To which I said, 'In that case we'll go privately; how quick would that be?' When he said, 'a couple of hours', I said, 'Let's do it.' The doctor looked doubtful and asked if she could afford it. 'Well, we will afford it,' I reassured him.

Of course, Sarah could not afford the treatment. She owed money to every shop in Elizabeth Street, just around the corner from her flat. I started to ring around the family and had some difficult conversations. I knew there was a trust fund in her favour, but it would not be paid to her unless she was entirely rehabilitated. If she was not, the fund would eventually be divided among the rest of the family. I made the argument to everyone that we should all relinquish our right to the trust money so that Sarah could have her operation. This went down fine with most members of the family, but not with some others. Nevertheless, we raised the money.

Sarah's liver deteriorated inexorably as time passed. By 1982, she had been fading significantly for months. When I went to see her during yet another period of hospitalisation, it was clear that she would not recover. She was only sixty-seven, but alcohol had inevitably taken its toll. 'I do not want to die here. I want to go home.' I took her home that afternoon.

A nurse was installed in her flat, and her doctor, who was the prison doctor that she had met and made friends with while she was in Holloway, would come to visit. They had stayed in touch after her release from prison and used to go out drinking together.

After a few difficult days during which there was no change I called the doctor 'She's extremely uncomfortable. Can you give her something to take away the pain?' He agreed and wrote a prescription. I went around the corner to the chemist in Elizabeth Street, but they said they could not provide the medication, as it was a dangerous drug and that I would have to go to John Bell and Croyden in Wigmore Street. I got in my car and drove there, only to find that the only pharmacist who could dispense this particular medicine was not there at the time and I would have to wait.

Eventually, after what seemed like an eternity, I was given the medicine and set off back to Eaton Square. I got as far as St James's Square when I was blocked by a demonstration of nurses protesting along Pall Mall. How ironic that nurses were impeding my mercy run.

I was so distraught that I just put my head in my hands and cried. A policeman came up to the car and asked me what the matter was. I said, probably dropping a few biographical details, that I was trying to get deliver medicine my aunt who was very ill. 'Don't worry,' said the policeman, 'we'll escort you.' So, with sirens blaring, I was fast-tracked to Eaton Square.

The medicine had an instant effect on Sarah. it was absolutely wonderful; she was transformed. She had not had a drink for months but now she said she would love to have some oysters, washed down with Chablis. I rang up Wheelers' Oyster Bar and ordered a delivery. Sarah then started calling her friends all over the world. I did not realise it at the time, but she was saying goodbye.

One of her closest friends and confidants was the Welsh pianist, Idris Evans, who had often accompanied her and played at the Café Royal. In 1974, they had performed together at a concert in Israel in aid of children from both sides who had been caught in the crossfire of the Arab Israeli War.

Idris came that afternoon and sat down at the piano, which stood by the window in her basement sitting room. Sarah's bedroom was on the ground floor, so he opened the door to the garden so that she could hear him sing and play, which he did very loudly. It was lovely, especially as she had written some of the songs herself. One of the lines was, 'Though I lose you I'll hold on to the dream.' It was a line from a song Sarah had composed while she was playing in Shakespeare's *As You Like It*. The producer gave her permission to sing it to her father who was in the audience. The nurse said that when Sarah heard the song, she smiled faintly, but then fell back into a coma and never opened her eyes again.

I had given Sarah a second dose of the medicine, by the time the doctor rang to see how she was. I said, 'Marvellous! That medicine is absolute magic, but there's only one dose left. Can you bring another prescription?' He said, 'I think, Celia, you'll find that's quite sufficient.' Sarah then had the third dose, at which point the nurse said, 'I do not think she's going to last very long.'

Sarah died shortly afterwards. She was an incredibly generous and lovely person and I adored her.

The funeral was very poignant; so much talent so much vitality, so much sadness. What was really nice was that on the day of the service, at St Michael's, Chester Square, all the shops in Elizabeth Street closed, because all the owners and the staff wanted to attend. That was particularly touching particularly as she owed most of them money. Although she was often a nuisance to them when she was drunk, they still really liked her, because she was a truly lovely person.

15

A General's Wife's

In April 1985, when Ken and I got back from our visit with British Aerospace to Pakistan, it was clear that what had been a working relationship had turned into something different. I was forty-two years old but although Ken was seventeen years my senior, I had no doubts. We decided we wanted to spend our future together. In June he moved into my flat in Warwick Square and we were married five weeks later.

They say, 'marry in haste, repent at leisure', but my marriage to Ken was the one that lasted the longest, over twenty years, during which time we were extremely happy. He was very different from almost all the other men I had met in my life; something of a renaissance man from a very different background.

Born the son of a gardener in a farm-worker's cottage in Newhaven, his mother took in lodgers to make ends meet. An elementary, then grammar school education, where he excelled as a rugby player and an athlete, won him a place in the Royal Artillery in 1944 and on the university short course at Oxford. He missed the Second World War by a whisker but was commissioned in 1946 and was a young officer during the messy end of Britain's mandate in Palestine.

When war broke out between the new state of Israel and its Arab neighbours, he commanded a troop of 7th Field Artillery on the Great Bitter Lake in Egypt. Described by a colleague as 'a soldiers' soldier' he spent most of his career in troubled war zones. He rose through the ranks to become a major-general with more ribbons on his chest than any soldier of his generation. He became an army flyer and won a DFC and an MBE in flying over two hundred sorties in the Korean War and flew missions in the Malayan Emergency. He also served in Northern Ireland and, later in life, was made a Companion of the Bath. This final honour, pretty well automatic unlike the two earlier ones, of which he was very proud, he would have said, 'came with the rations'.

Perhaps his greatest honour had come in 1975, when he was made Commander of the Sultan of Oman's Armed Forces. Often leading attacks, on one occasion, he became involved in a mortar bombardment in South Yemen, when everyone around him seemed to be running for cover. Not in the slightest disconcerted, Ken called out to his ADC, 'Don't run! Generals don't run; just walk briskly.'

He was very popular with the men who had served under his command which was clearly demonstrated at his funeral when former colleagues came from as far away as Hong Kong to pay their respects.

Ken was much more than a soldier. He captained his regimental boxing team, had several of his paintings exhibited in the Royal Academy and for a number of years became *The Sun* newspaper's defence adviser. He wrote his life story, *A Fortunate Soldier* and *Khalida,* a novel based on his experiences in the military, especially his time in the Middle East. He embarked on this when the Ministry of Defence, who had to approve the book, censored some of, in his opinion, the most interesting stories so he decided to put them in a novel.

More important than any of the above derring-do and professional gifts, were Ken's personal qualities. Despite his achievements, he was an extremely modest and generous man, a devoted father, and a marvellous husband. Everyone liked him.

He had three daughters who adored their father and gave me a wonderful welcome into the family. The two eldest, Mo and Jane were busy with their children but came to visit us as often as they could. Nicky, who had just got married, spent a lot of time with us and she and I became very good friends. Ken was very proud of them all.

We were married amidst the towering Doric columns of the lovely registry office at Old Marylebone Town Hall, where pop stars like Paul McCartney married two of his wives, and where Ringo Starr tied the knot with Barbara Bach. We did not have rows of photographers on stepladders to snap us, or hordes of screaming fans on the steps to greet us, but it was a special occasion with family and friends. I wore a pretty blue silk dress decorated with red hearts; definitely more attractive than my last wedding outfit.

The day was not completely drama free. We had decided on a dinner for seventy of our closest family and friends at my Warwick Square flat. I made what I thought were the perfect preparations, but when the caterer, Searcy's, supposedly the best in the business, brought the china, it had black rims. I was not best pleased. I told them that if they did not appear immediately and change them for gold-rimmed plates more appropriate for a wedding than a funeral, I would throw the whole lot out of the window, one plate at a time. They came around almost immediately.

We did not have our honeymoon until September, when we went to my father and stepmother's lovely house in the Algarve in Portugal. The last time I had been there was with my brother, Julian, to collect my father when he had had a stroke. The memories were not good, but we had a very nice few days. I then discovered that I was having a miscarriage. Remembering from my father's illness what the hospitals were like, I told Ken that we had to get out of the country immediately. We dashed to the airport and I was wheel-chaired back to London. It was a miserable journey, but there was a silver-lining to the awful experience; at forty-two, I was still able to conceive.

Within a few months I was pregnant again, with Alexander, who was born the following August. The whole episode was appalling, almost like a delivery from the Middle Ages. When I was first pregnant, as a humorous gesture, Justin had given me a book called, *Childbirth in Later Years*, but my ordeal was far from amusing.

The pregnancy went badly from the start. We had gone to Queen Charlotte's, which was then in Hammersmith, and considered the best place for maternity care for what was I thought, rather unattractively, called geriatric mothers. I should have left the obstetrician early on as I never liked him. At one appointment he took my blood pressure and found it a little high. Implying that he was fearfully attractive, he said, 'Perhaps I'll get my nurse to take it next time. It might not rise so high.'

It was not an easy pregnancy. At one stage I had a rash and was told I had German Measles. I said that I could clearly remember having had German Measles in Italy, so it seemed highly unlikely. Even so, it was early on in my pregnancy, so clearly a worry. They did a test, which showed I did have German measles and that an abortion was clearly the necessary option. Before the procedure I asked for another blood test and the results were quite different. The original test had apparently been switched with somebody else's by mistake.

If I had taken the medical advice, I could have aborted Alexander, but, fortunately, my stubbornness paid off and catastrophe was averted. Soon after I started to have problems and it seemed I might miscarry again. It was as if my body had, after the fifteen years since Dominic was born, forgotten what to do. Ken was in India much of the time and I would be in hospital on my own. I remember a nurse, referring to my age, saying derisively, 'Do you really want this baby?'

The actual birth was horrendous. Labour started and then stopped. The doctor came and said, 'We'd better do something to induce this baby' and proceeded to shove his fist inside me and give a brutal twist. As he did it, I was reminded of seeing the vet do something similar to a cow on our farm when I was a child. Of course, contractions started instantly. I rang for the nurse and asked if I could go to the labour ward. To my horror, she said, 'No, I'm afraid it's full now. You'll have to wait here.'

Finally, I was given an epidural. Things continued, then they said the baby was in distress, but there was no sign of the doctor. The anaesthetist vanished; he had gone home just as the pain kicked in again. The obstetrician was doing a caesarean, so he was not there either. Fortunately, nature took its course and Alexander arrived despite all attempts by the medical team to prevent it happening. Ken was with me throughout and said that what he had seen in the delivery room was worse than anything he had seen on the battlefield.

As for the anaesthetist as he was not there for the delivery, he did not send his bill. In response to my letter of complaint the obstetrician wrote, 'What are you complaining about? You had a live baby.'

After the birth, we stayed for a while in Warwick Square. But Ken said he wanted a real house with its own front door. So, without ever putting it on the market, we sold the flat to my father and stepmother and moved to a beautiful house in Kew. Although it was a lovely house, right on Kew Green with its picturesque cricket ground in the middle, I found the area far less appealing. It was for me, alone all day with a new baby, very isolating.

Perhaps I should have chosen Barnes, a much livelier place. I have often thought that, had I done so, I might still be living there. In any case, even before we had finished making the Kew house our own, we decided we wanted to live in the country. Before long we moved again, this time to Chieveley, near Newbury, to a beautiful Queen Anne vicarage which was something of a compromise location because Ken was working in London less than an hour away.

I wanted to re-use some of the curtains I had had made for Kew, so I went to the curtain makers who had made my curtains for years and asked for them to be let out by three inches, only to be told it would cost £750, which is what they cost in the first place! So, thinking it ridiculous, I decided to alter them myself; It took me all of an hour and a half. Emboldened by that, even though Chieveley was a big house with big windows, I decided to make all the curtains and bought myself an industrial machine. This was quite a challenge as I was pregnant again and Alexander, who was one year old, loved crawling under the curtains which I was making on the floor.

Houses have been very prominent in my life. In all, I have bought and sold twenty-eight of them, which, of course, is fifty-six transactions and all the tedious paraphernalia, legal and logistical, that goes with house moving. For several years, buying houses, doing them up and selling them was the way I made a living. After a while, Justin and Dominic became annoyed at having to keep their room looking perfect and the endless upheaval of moving house.

In the summer of 1987 Ken managed to get himself made redundant from British Aerospace. We decided to move again, this time into real countryside and looked to the West Country.

At that moment, to my delight, I discovered that I was pregnant again. One day when I was about eight weeks pregnant and house hunting in Devon, we went into a pub so that I could call the doctor and find out the results of the test I had just taken.

When I came out of the phone box with tears pouring down my face Ken immediately assumed the worst. But I was crying because I was told I was having a girl. I had felt sure it was going to be a fourth boy, but at long last, and approaching forty-five years of age, I was going to have a girl.

Having had a traumatic miscarriage before Alexander, endured such a terrifying experience giving birth to him, and realising that this was probably my last opportunity, I immediately chose a wonderful new doctor and more or less invalided myself for the next seven months.

My stepmother, Marie-Claire, wanted to know what sex the baby was, but when I refused to tell her, she said, 'I think you ought to tell your father, because he won't be alive to see his new grandchild.' I did tell him and sadly she was right. My father had never really recovered from the stroke he suffered in Portugal and died in November 1987 and was very never able to meet his granddaughter.

Ken and I had looked at various houses but had not found anything we really wanted. Then one day we turned up late in the evening at a house near Bampton, north of Tiverton and not far from the Exmoor National Park. It was a lovely Georgian manor house; we loved it straight away. Somehow, we had failed to notice a small lodge at the gate, which had been sold off separately to a former army officer who had coincidentally been under Ken's command in Oman.

It was not until we moved in, that we discovered a notice by the lodge that had been covered over. We removed the cover, to read a sign pronouncing, 'The Garden is Closed Today'. Without realising it, we had bought a very important garden of about fifteen acres and another ten acres of lovely woodland. We were told that it had more varieties of shrub than almost any other garden in England! It was incredible, but we could not maintain it. The best we could do was keep the grass and weeds down by cutting swathes through it with a small Kubota tractor.

We moved there in the January of 1988 and Sophie was born in May, on my 45th birthday. After Alexander's horrendous delivery, I had sworn that I would never again put myself or my child through a similar experience and that if ever it happened again, I would have a caesarean. So, in the incredibly luxurious Portland Hospital near Regents Park Sophie arrived safely and without stress, as planned. No stress for me but it was different for Ken who unlike me had no screen to shield him from what was happening. Typically, he could not resist being on the front line and had to be caught by the nurses as he keeled over.

After Alexander, I had been so exhausted that there would be days when I would not get dressed at all. Ken was marvellous and would come home and take over. By the time I had Sophie, my body was back into maternal mode and I found it far easier with her. Perhaps the secret was that I rested in the Portland for twelve days after she arrived.

Every morning I asked the consultant, 'Are you sure the insurance will pay?' and he said, 'No problem.' Mercifully, late motherhood then became a dream and was a wonderful time. I can see myself now: Sophie under one arm, and Alexander running around whilst I stirred the food on the Aga; happy days!

It was at this time that I got to know Robert, Tim to his friends, who in my opinion got the closest to the subject in his portrayal of my grandfather. Edwina and I had decided that it would be fun to make a musical about our grandfather. She had two friends, a director, Robin Hardy, who was no relation to Robert and Rex Berry, a producer. We all got together, and *Winnie* was born. Tim Hardy was of course cast in the leading role with Virginia McKenna as Clementine.

Winnie opened at the Victoria Palace theatre in the third week of May 1988 one week after my daughter Sophie was born. If the members of the Women's Voluntary Service had been representative of the country *Winnie* would have been a great hit. However, it soon became clear that we did not have the financial backing to get us through the initial few weeks and establish the production which closed after six weeks. The demise of *Winnie* was a disappointing but not one that I could dwell on with a new baby taking over my life. The best thing that resulted from my foray into the theatre was my friendship with Tim Hardy who remained one of my closest friends for the next thirty years. He was a regular visitor and whenever we moved to a new house, Ken and I moved six times in twenty years, I would always take him to the local shops where he would be instantly recognised either as Siegfried from *All Creatures Great and Small* or as Winston Churchill from the *Wilderness Years*. This was very good for my street cred and laid the grounds for excellent service. We established a tradition that Tim and my aunt Mary would spend New Year's Eve with us in Wiltshire. This was a very happy arrangement enjoyed by all. Tim was Alexander's very attentive and caring godfather. He would sweep him into the Savernake Forest to hunt rabbits with bows and arrows. Not any old bows and arrows. Tim's came from the wreck of the *Mary Rose* the raising of which he had been a major player. During the last few years of his life, we had great enjoyment doing readings of the letters of Winston and Clementine.

During the interval on that first night of *Winnie*, someone in the loo looked me up and down and asked, 'Oh, congratulations, when is it due?' Not what you want to hear in your mid-forties when you have just given birth!

The next five years of effectively 'dropping out' and 'playing babies' in Devon were the most idyllic of my life. We had no money, but we were totally happy. I had never wanted to have nannies because I had loved my nanny so much and I did not want to be in a competition for my children's love. When Dominic and Justin were small, and I was working, I did have help most of the time but never anyone who became important in their lives.

I had one nanny who, the minute Justin met her, he said he would get rid of her in a week. It took him two weeks; she had worked for King Hussein and was used to being waited on and also hopeless with the boys. When I told her to leave her son called me and begged me to keep her on. I then found an old-fashioned nanny who looked after Dominic for a while. She was very nice despite being quite grand. She had worked for the Begum Aga Khan. Another was a very lovely girl from Columbia who was with us when we were burgled. When the police interviewed her, they asked if I realised that I had an underage girl looking after my children. I had no idea that she was only fifteen. In Devon I had Mrs Blake, who was a wonderful woman. She did the cleaning but most importantly was very good with Alexander and Sophie. Her husband, Gordon, was quite a rogue and did the outside jobs.

Neither of us were working during our early years in Devon. Ken wrote his autobiography, *A Fortunate Soldier*, and we did occasional bed and breakfast through a company called Country Homes and Castles. The house was perfect for it. It was painted white, with a very lovely view looking down the valley. It had a big stable block where I made some flats. Not quite as pretty as the house in Chieveley, but it had all the space we needed and a wonderful view and a beautiful walled garden.

Over two and a half years, a number of interesting characters came to stay. There was an American film director who arrived with his much younger girlfriend. I had been sent a message the evening before from the agency warning me that he was very upset at an earlier B and B where he had complained. 'No lady, no soup, no salad and just plonk.' So, I really felt I had to push the boat out. We were going to make sure we had good wine, salad, and soup with 'the lady' very much in evidence!

I rang a friendly neighbour nearby and asked to borrow his cook who I knew was very good. We were only four for dinner, but I decided to have Mrs Blake come and serve us. Her twelve-year-old daughter, Marianne helped her, so we were somewhat overstaffed prompting our guest to remark, 'Where's the tweeny?' We did apparently pass the test.

I thought we had blown it when, before dinner, I went into the drawing room and found his petite and stick-thin girlfriend, who worked for Saks, Fifth Avenue, cowering in a wingback chair while Obby, our Golden retriever, one paw on each wing, was humping her. He was about the same size as her and she was clearly terrified. I was surprised she apparently hadn't reported it otherwise we would certainly have heard from the agency. The next guests were a group of Italians who were enormous fun.

We did not do much more but on another occasion my friend Linda Duncan, who has a travel agency in Oklahoma, sent me three wonderful women. She said, 'I have three widows who want to stay for five days and need a car and a chauffeur.' Linda asked me if I wanted her to organise the transport, but I said that we could deal with it. We used our car and Ken, and I were the drivers. We met the widows at the airport, and I found some local bachelors to entertain them. We invited the baronet who was living in the flat in our stables, his title greatly impressed them, a charming local estate agent and our neighbour, Guy Dennler, who not only lent me his cook but gave a dinner party in their honour. So, all went well, and the merry widows, who were delightful, had a wonderful time and went home full of stories of English hospitality.

The B and B would have made money if we had done it regularly, but as we were doing it more for fun than profit, it was not a particularly thriving business. Eventually and reluctantly, we realised that we could not let the wonderful garden, that we had unknowingly acquired with the house to go wild from neglect and we could not afford the two full time gardeners we would have needed to maintain it. Therefore, in 1991, we decided to move. again, this time to a very rural thatched farmhouse in Carscombe, a small village a few miles away where we stayed for another two years.

Alexander particularly enjoyed it there. He still remembers the 'wild woods', and the local farmer's sheep and horses in our fields. It was at Carscombe that Ken became defence adviser to *The Sun* and the children started school. Ken became very busy and one day I came home from a visit to London expecting to find him and the children, a fire going, and dinner cooked. But the house was empty and there was a note on the table saying he had been called away and the children were with Mrs Blake. It was obvious that we had to move closer to London.

We sold Carscombe and rented a cottage near Hungerford, from Johnny Morris, whose children's television programme, *Animal Magic*, was so popular on in the sixties and seventies.

We had already made up our minds that we wanted to send Alexander and Sophie to a Co-Ed school and decided on Marlborough College in Wiltshire. After a long search we found what we wanted in the Savernake Forest a ten-minute drive from Marlborough. This became my most ambitious house project. I mentioned that I was looking for an architect and three friends who did not know each other said they knew one who would be perfect. A week later three brochures came in the post all from the same architect, Roderick James the timber-framed barn specialist. A few years later he would restore Windsor Castle after the fire, and we could never have afforded him. His magic transformed a two-up, two-down country cottage into a large oak-framed house with tennis court and croquet lawn. Everyone thought I had gone mad because they had seen the lovely houses I had had before. The front always looked small and one guest's chauffeur was reluctant to drop him off because he thought such a small place could not possibly be the right address. Nevertheless, we were very happy there for fifteen years.

We became short of money in Wiltshire. It may not have shown outwardly, but it did in the bank balance. Basically, Ken was living on his pension, and I was speaking anywhere and everywhere for anyone who would pay me. The rewards were not generous, and I hated leaving the children, but it had to be done, otherwise the school fees could not have been paid.

On her death bed, my great friend Rachel Ford wrote a cheque for Alexander's school fees. She loved me, and she loved boys, but was less interested in girls, so, sadly, she did not do the same for Sophie. Luckily, Bedwyn was close enough to Marlborough which meant it was possible for the children eventually to go there as day pupils, so Rachel's wonderful legacy covered most of the school fees.

One night, the children's prep school headmaster and his wife came to dinner at Bedwyn and she admired our Herend china. As soon as she sat down, she said, 'It's so pretty!' The day before I had broken a Waterford wine glass. I had called Thomas Goode in Mayfair and asked how much it would cost to replace it and was told they were £120 each, which I thought ridiculously expensive. We used the china and glasses perhaps three times a year and it was not possible to put them in the dishwasher. So, realising that our guest was very envious of them, I worked out their value and said, 'If we don't have to pay school fees for two years, you can take them away; they're yours.' The deal was done and all parties very satisfied.

One day I came home to find a bizarre-looking television interviewer in the house. He wore a shiny shell suit, and his fingers were festooned with gold rings. I knew that Ken had been asked to appear on a programme which would appeal to younger viewers, but I was taken aback to hear him being asked if he had ever thought of supporting Hitler!

Only later did we realise that the interviewer was Sacha Baron Cohen's notorious character, Ali G, who was doing a recording for his 'Innit' Christmas special. Ken had trusted the producer, someone who had he worked with before and had been very professional, so Ali G's somewhat perverse questions came as a bit of a shock, especially when he asked Ken about 'Batty boys' in the army and if he had ever considered changing sides. In fact, Ken came out if it very well, especially compared to some of the other interviewees whom Ali G had completely bamboozled.

In mid-1996, when Ken was defence adviser to *The Sun*, during an idle conversation about politics with John Kay, his friendly contact on the paper, I suggested that they should run a column in the build up to the forthcoming election written by a 'Floating Voter' and that I would like to do it. John was intrigued by the idea but said that I would need to persuade his colleagues that, bearing in mind my Conservative connections and background, I really was undecided in my voting intentions. I was grilled by two or three people and passed the test. The Sun's Floating Voter was born.

I wrote a few articles during the next year and was really enjoying the prospect of the election which was not far off. I decided that I must formalise my arrangements with the paper and called the editor who was very amenable and asked me to send him a fax laying out my proposal. This I did immediately and ten minutes later it came back with a one-word answer 'agreed' and his signature.

A few days later the General Election was announced, and I was astounded to read the headline in *The Sun*, 'We are going for Blair.' Of course, I immediately telephoned the editor and asked what his floating voter was meant to do? He replied, 'can you edge towards Blair?' I said I could not because the whole point was that I truly had not decided whether I would vote Labour, Liberal or Conservative, or whether I would vote at all. I explained how much I had wanted to do the column, how disappointed I was and that if I had dreamed that this could happen, I would have gone to another paper. 'Send me your bill', was all he said. This I did charging at the established rate for what he had agreed I should do.

He complained that it was too high and balked at paying for, 'work I hadn't done.' I then asked the advice of an acquaintance who was in the newspaper world and was told, 'write a friendly letter saying how much you wanted to do it and that he had agreed to your terms but in the middle drop in an unmistakable legalistic phrase.' This I did with help from a barrister friend and immediately received a cheque for the full amount. This was, in the circumstances, a good outcome but a big disappointment.

When Alexander and Sophie were at Marlborough, we never missed their rugby, netball, or tennis matches. One day, Alexander was playing tennis with his partner, James Middleton, when a very charming man sat down next to us. He said he had heard me on the radio. Ken looked at me quizzically, and I whispered, 'Father of the future Queen!' 'What Queen?' Ken asked, in a whisper too loud not to be overheard. From that day I decided whispering was not a good idea as his hearing wasn't as good as it had been.

The first twelve or thirteen years of our marriage were very happy but there was a storm approaching. Ken was fifty-nine when we married but stayed fit and healthy. However, little by little he had developed a few issues which were finally diagnosed as Parkinson's disease. He was reluctant to take his medication as he had heard that it would only work for a few years and he wanted to save it for later. I tried to persuade him that it would be better to have a few good years now, while it could be effective and that probably another remedy would come along. He did not agree, and life became difficult. Eventually, although we never stopped loving each other, in 2006, we agreed to part. Ken died in 2009 at the age of eighty-three. Of course, if we had known that this was going to happen, we would have stayed together.

One day a policewoman turned up at my front door and, as they always do on television, asked if she could come in and suggested that I sit down. Telling Alexander and Sophie that the father they adored had died was the worst thing I have ever had to do. Especially as it was completely unexpected.

He had walked into Boots chemist in Marlborough, fell to the floor and died instantly which was a good way to go for him but a terrible shock for everyone else. Ken would have appreciated his friend, Ian Sprackling's observation in the eulogy at the funeral, 'Ken always said he wanted to die with his boots on.' We were very lucky to have had him.

16

A Little Box of Treasures

When Alexander and Sophie started school and Ken was busy writing and working with *The Sun*, I began to have some spare time available and started to think about what I was going to do as the children got older and more independent.

In 1993 I went to see my cousin, Peregrine Churchill, the son of my grandfather's brother, Jack. He had just turned eighty and lived in Hampshire. When we sat down to tea, I noticed a somewhat battered tin trunk on the table beside us. Curious, I asked what it was, and Peregrine immediately suggested that we should have a look. I think he had put it there deliberately to stir my imagination.

Despite his arthritis, he managed to get down on the floor, where, like a pair of inquisitive children, we proceeded to rummage through what turned out to be a most amazing little box of treasures. Peregrine's father, Jack, who had been the solid member of the family and had been the executor of several wills, had kept numerous family documents. In that tin trunk between us on the floor was a collection of diaries and letters which would set my life on an entirely new direction.

It was an extraordinary find. There were, amongst other things, my great-grandmother's diaries and my grandfather's childhood letters. It was a really amazing assortment of riches that were not only of great family importance, but also things of considerable historical interest.

I was enchanted and with no ulterior motive said, 'Someone should do something with these.' To which he said, 'You do it' and pushed the box over to me. That was the beginning of the rest of my life.

I drove home, called Edwina, and said, 'I'm going to write a book, do you know any publishers?' She said she knew Nicholas Thompson at Heinemann. I rang him the next morning, which was a Tuesday, and told him what I planned to do. His reply was a little disconcerting, 'You will have to be quick; I'm retiring on Friday!'

Despite his imminent departure an appointment was made for Thursday and I rushed around trying to put together some photographs and copies of some of the letters. It was not the most immaculate book proposal ever presented, partly because I had very little time, but mainly because I had no idea what such a thing should look like.

I made the presentation and, the following day, Nicholas signed his last book contract. The die was cast, I was an author, perhaps not fully fledged, but I was certainly a newly born fledgling. The easiest part of the deal was deciding what I was going to write. The choice was made for me by the contents of the box. Easily the most memorable bundles were my grandfather's letters, some of them tear-stained, written when he was a little boy. I decided I would tell the story of his early life.

The contents of the box were placed in the Churchill Archives at Churchill College Cambridge, but I was allowed the first run at them. My uncle Randolph, who wrote the first two volumes of my grandfather's biography before Martin Gilbert took over, had dealt with some of the early life, but not in great depth, so I had reasonably uncharted territory to explore.

Understandably, the conservators at Cambridge have the responsibility to preserve documents for posterity and immediately copied everything and put the originals into safe storage. However, I had had the opportunity to handle them well over a century after they were written; tear-stained letters from a lonely little schoolboy that told of the early years of his long and extraordinary life.

For me, they offered the prospect of a very personal and emotional journey of my own. It was exciting and I could not wait to start. Apart from his own account, *My Early Life*, I was about to open a completely new chapter in the life of a man about whom more has been written than almost anyone else.

Everything moved very quickly. The renowned literary agent, Ed Victor, took me on. I got up early every morning and sat and pored over the copies of the letters, took my children to school, then settled down again to do more work. Of particular importance for me was the fact that Alexander and Sophie were a similar age to my grandfather when he wrote his letters, so I was able to share their fascination with the contents.

At times, it was heartrending for me. I knew my grandfather when he was a lovable old man, a man who had achieved so much, who everyone greatly admired. Now I was able to get to know him all over again; this time as a boy who was dismissed as having few prospects and whose parents failed to give him the attention he craved. I went to his old schools. At St George's School at Ascot, they managed to find some school reports and an interesting letter from a German school friend. At Harrow, there had to be a meeting of the board of governors to sanction the release of the details of when he was flogged. This seemed a bit over the top, but permission was granted. The whole process was remarkably straightforward, and it all fell into place very well. *From Winston With a Love and Kisses*, was published in 1994 by Sinclair-Stevenson. My agent, Ed Victor, achieved a serialisation in the *Daily Mail*, for which they paid very well and found an American publisher. The book launch was at The Cabinet War Rooms.

I had not thought any further ahead, but it did not take long to decide to continue my grandfather's story. *Love and Kisses* was going to be published in South Africa, so Ken and I planned a holiday there with the children, when I could also research my next venture. Having examined my grandfather's life from birth until he left Sandhurst in 1894, I wanted to look at his life from then until his marriage to my grandmother in 1908, during which time his thrilling adventures in South Africa in the Boer War were for me the most fascinating and exciting.

When we arrived in Johannesburg, I was scheduled to go straight into an interview about the book on South African television and then to the launch party. On the way, I discovered that the publisher had only ordered three hundred copies for the whole country. Realising that the intended conversation about *Love and Kisses* was a complete waste of time, I took the interviewer to one side and suggested we change the purpose of the conversation. I asked if I could make an appeal to the public for any descendants of people who knew my grandfather during the Boer War. She clearly found that more interesting than talking about my book and made a very strong appeal on my behalf.

After the launch party we went back to Mary Oppenheimer's house, where we were staying. I had given Mary's telephone number on air, and by the time we got back, there had been sixty telephone calls. I realised straight away that there would be sufficient material in South Africa to forget the whole fourteen years between Sandhurst and marriage and focus my next book on the nine months of his time in the Boer War. My journey to my second book, *Churchill, Wanted Dead or Alive*, had begun. This was not just a catchy title but the name of the game that my brother and sister and I had played when we were children.

I had plenty of time to do the research and write the book, as I wanted it to coincide with the centenary of the Anglo-Boer War in 1899. In Ken, who had written books of his own, I had a resident researcher and editor, who was enormously important to my writing. Not only that but, when it came to all things military, which played a major role throughout my grandfather's entire life, I had on hand a major general, who really enjoyed making sure I got the military/political context correct in everything I wrote. During three trips to South Africa, I spent six months criss-crossing the country meeting an array of people who were the custodians of family stories about my grandfather. This led to some bizarre encounters and some wonderful new friends. On one occasion, I got a call from a man who said he had a photograph taken by his father when he was imprisoned with my grandfather in Pretoria. I immediately rushed to see him at his home in a rather seedy part of Durban. He lived in a block of flats, so Ken waited in the car with the children while I got into the lift, in which an argument was in progress between two call girls and their pimp. When I knocked on the door, a very eccentric-looking man opened it, dressed in a grubby string vest with a parrot on his shoulder. When, with great pride, he showed me his photograph, it was immediately obvious that not only was the person in question not my grandfather, it was not even taken during the Boer War. It was an image of a First World War despatch rider. I thanked the man profusely, promised to return the photograph after having it checked by military experts and managed to get away unscathed, if a little unnerved.

Altogether this was a more complicated book than *Love and Kisses*, which was built on a straightforward chronology of letters. In *Wanted Dead or Alive*, I had to piece together a jigsaw puzzle of stories from different people in different places, talking about a series of different events. It was living research and I absolutely loved it. What a real treat it was to travel the country and meet both Boer and British South Africans, who had all these fascinating accounts of my grandfather when he was an impetuous and hugely ambitious young man, aged just twenty-five. In many cases, their stories had never been told before.

I had some wonderful help from the South African guide and historian, Ken Gillings, who found the grandson of the man in charge of the Boer prison where my grandfather was incarcerated. He unearthed the descendants of the engine driver of the armoured train my grandfather was travelling in when it was ambushed by the Boers. Perhaps most intriguingly, he found family members of the mine manager at Witbank who, in miraculous circumstances after he had escaped from prison, hid him down his mine and of the man who had smuggled Winston, hidden in bales of wool, onto a train going to Portuguese East Africa and freedom. All three of them were founts of knowledge who helped me create what was, in effect, a real *Boy's Own* adventure story. Not only was it a pilgrimage in my grandfather's footsteps, I was also re-living history. I was listening to stories and hearing accounts, standing in the very places where he stood and where I could visualise everything in vivid detail. What was most striking in talking to the custodians of family memories, is that those he met, even though he was so young, seemed to know that they should remember what he did and what he said.

Writing books opened another adventure in my life, one which I approached with considerable trepidation. While I was writing *Love and Kisses*, I was asked by Richard Langworth the founder of the International Churchill Society to go to Washington to speak about the book. I had always loathed speaking in public and could not think of a more daunting prospect. However, I had a reason to wriggle out, arguing that I did not want to speak about the book before it was published. But, to my horror, he was persistent and said, 'Well, why don't you just come and introduce your cousin, Winston, who is speaking.' Thankfully, that was two minutes, not a full speech, so I felt sure I could manage that.

Anyway, I must have done a reasonable job, because I was then asked to be the keynote speaker at dinner at the Society's next conference in Calgary, Canada. Without thinking of the consequences, I said, yes. Not only that, they then said, they wanted forty-five minutes. I was horrified! Then it got even worse when I discovered that my Aunt Mary was going to be there. The prospect of speaking in public was one thing but I never like having members of my family in the audience, especially, as in Mary's case, the member of the family who knew more about my subject than I did.

At dinner I was seated between the British consul general and the chairman of the society. Both men sensed that I was nervous and were very sympathetic. I did not touch a drop of alcohol, or any kind of drink, for fear of needing the loo halfway through. I could not eat a morsel, as my nerves had extinguished any need or desire for food. I was scheduled to speak at nine o'clock, but it was ten-thirty before I got to my feet. By then, the room was thick with tobacco smoke and my audience had been drinking since early evening. I felt like a lamb to the slaughter!

The room was long and thin, so I had to deliver my speech to an audience of three hundred like an umpire at a tennis match. What a nightmare. But it got worse. Within a minute or two, there was a bang, a crash, and a groan. A woman had fallen off her chair and collapsed on the floor. Now, I would know what to do, call a halt and summon medical help, but then, I just turned the opposite way and continued to address half of the audience. All the while, the paramedics tried to revive the stricken woman with mouth-to-mouth resuscitation before carrying her off to hospital. My first big speech certainly made an impression but not the one I had hoped for. A quarter of a century later I still meet people who were there, who immediately recount the tale with great glee. Strangely, it was helpful that it was so bad because I then took the view that if I could survive that, I could survive anything. The Calgary experience removed all fear of public speaking. So much so that I now do little else.

Shortly after Calgary, Ken's daughter, Mo, introduced me to a man who was apparently very well connected in Japan and could arrange some speaking engagements. Things moved fast and before long I found myself speaking in Korea and Japan and for the first time but having to speak through an interpreter. My first speech was to an audience of over two thousand, of whom, perhaps ten per cent could understand English. I found it very daunting and unrewarding to address an audience who could not react to what I said or laugh at my jokes until they were relayed to them by the interpreter.

The first speech was made very awkward when at the end a member of the audience came up to me and after saying that he had for some years worked at the British embassy asked if he could tell me something. I knew I was not going to like what was coming. He first said how nice it was that I had opened my speech greeting the audience in Japanese. That said, he hoped that I would not mind if he told me that, unfortunately, whoever had told me what to say spoke very vulgar Japanese. He also asked if I was aware that my agent, who had produced the 'vulgar' translation, had declined an invitation for me to dine with the most important people in the area. He said, 'the tables are laid, the food prepared, the presents are wrapped, and the Mayor is waiting to welcome you'.

Of course, I said immediately that I would be delighted to accept the invitation which had not been relayed to me. Realising that there were other invitations that had been turned down because there was no financial reward, I enquired what else had been refused. The next two days were very busy as, having already unknowingly caused offence, I decided to accept all invitations without exception. Following about ten visits, including schools, factories, war memorials and the local sewage works, I certainly left having learned a great deal about the region.

By the time we got to Tokyo, I realised that this particular business relationship must come to an end. My diplomatic friend took over and introduced me to a new agent and a publisher in Tokyo. By the end of this first visit to Japan, I had made friends with three people who would make future visits to Tokyo both easier and more enjoyable: the former diplomat who had become my adviser, my new interpreter and the head of the Japan–British Society.

With this new network in place, in no time, I was introduced to the manager of the Mitzukoshi store in Tokyo and talks started on putting on a Winston Churchill painting exhibition in three of its stores around the country. To my surprise, I discovered that the city had a 'Churchill Kai', The Churchill Club of Tokyo, a prestigious society of amateur painters. Having arranged the New York exhibit with Edwina ten years before, I knew the procedure and made arrangements with the National Trust at Chartwell, my grandparents' former home in Kent, which houses the largest collection of his paintings. I would need to travel to Tokyo every month during the six months before the exhibition to help with the planning. Virgin agreed to be one of the sponsors, thus solving the problem of shipping the paintings and my air travel. The only other sponsorship I found was Pol Roger which was happy to provide my grandfather's favourite champagne for the opening party.

As well as the paintings I took some other objects from Chartwell. At each store a conservator, appointed by the National Trust, had to check each item. As the exhibits were being set out in Tokyo, the conservator came up to me and said she had some very bad news and produced my grandfather's riding boots.

'They are very damaged and scratched.' She told me in an anguished tone. Indeed they were, but it was hardly surprising as he had worn them for years and they had aged accordingly. Another of the exhibits was a tear-stained letter that he had sent to his mother from school. This was travelling loose in an envelope and fortunately survived the journey. Soon after, with all the other precious documents at the Churchill Archives in Cambridge, it was micro-filmed and stored away. I was extremely lucky to be able to take all these wonderful objects without which the exhibition would not have been nearly as interesting.

After six months of planning, I arrived at the Mitzukoshi store in Tokyo to see the exhibition before it opened. I asked the manager if he had received the champagne for the party. He told me he had and took me to his office and showed me a pile of boxes. He was clearly astonished when I explained that they had to be cooled down to a suitable temperature before the Pol Roger agent who had provided them arrived at the party a few hours later. I refused to move until he had got them removed and taken to a cold room. I then told him that I would not open the exhibition until I had a glass of ice-cold champagne in my hand. In the land where the men are in charge and the women, on the surface are distinctly meek, this clearly shocked him.

I returned for the opening and as I approached the podium was offered a glass of champagne on a silver salver. It was of course lukewarm but there was nothing I could do but apologise to the agent and hope that he didn't report it back to the Pol Roger family who are very generous with their sponsorship but can surely expect their sparkling nectar to be served at the correct temperature. The annual Mitzukoshi exhibitions still take place to this day.

In the following years, I returned to Japan speak several times but never really felt comfortable having to have an interpreter when I spoke. Sadly, I never managed to travel to the famous places like Kyoto, as I always felt guilty whenever I went away and wanted to get back home to Ken and the children as soon as possible.

There was one final twist to the journey of *Churchill Wanted Dead or Alive*. There had been a film about my grandfather's early life, *Young Winston*, starring Simon Ward, released in 1972. However, it passed over his time in South Africa quite quickly. So, as soon as I had finished the book, I wanted to turn it into a film. Through some deft footwork and a dose of good fortune, I managed to get an appointment with Bob Iger, the president of Disney in Los Angeles. When I walked in, I found pictures of my grandfather all over the walls of his office. I immediately thought I was on to a winner. So, I made my *Wanted Dead or Alive* pitch, to which he said he loved it, but, regretted that Disney no longer made films like it anymore. What a disappointment!

After *Wanted Dead or Alive*, I planned to do a third book. It would be about my grandfather's travels. Again, it would involve living research: travelling, meeting people, doing detective work, and piecing together a jigsaw of a storyline. Not only that, I had travelled with him myself, so I had a head start. I needed a good title, because I felt *Love and Kisses* and *Wanted Dead or Alive* were really excellent titles and I wanted another one to complete the trio. I was speaking in Cleveland Ohio when the man who was introducing me got up and said, 'Celia has been chasing Churchill all around the world' Perfect! I had my title.

Chasing Churchill was, in some ways, a much bigger task. It was to cover many places and tell stories over a much longer period of time. Again, I wanted to stay away from the much-told events of his career as a political leader and his exploits in war. My focus was on his passion for travel and the huge number of places he visited all over the world. I wanted to explore his lifelong attachment to the United States, the birthplace of his mother and, in particular, his love of painting, which became an ever more important source of solace in his life. From that moment research took up most of our family holidays. Since my grandfather liked to travel to places that were 'batheable and paintable' it was no hardship. Sometimes we would be driving through France or Italy and I would see a sign to somewhere that he had painted which meant our journeys were full of diversions. After many holidays like this Alexander's and Sophie asked, 'Please may we have a non-Churchill holiday for a change?'

I also had other invaluable resources available to me in the form of people who were still alive who served with my grandfather during the war. Two of his wonderful secretaries, Patrick Kinna and Elizabeth Layton who were both at his side at home and abroad for most of the war were really keen to help me and became great friends. Richard Langworth, the head of the International Churchill Society, was planning to lead a tour to South Africa to coincide with the centenary of the Boer War in July 1999. As soon as he advertised it, he found that he had a conflicting engagement, so he asked if I would take it over. As I love South Africa, I was delighted and, having just published *Churchill Wanted Dead or Alive*, I knew that, with the help of all the people I had met during my research trips, I could make a successful and interesting tour.

Ken was thrilled at the prospect and we set off with Alexander and Sophie to find a tour operator and plan the itinerary. As usual, basing ourselves with my friend Mary Oppenheimer, we turned the venture into a wonderful family holiday.

There was no shortage of candidates who wanted to come. That was just as well, as, for logistic reasons, we needed to fill a forty-four-seater plane for part of the tour and any fewer people would have made it financially unworkable. I found that there was one tour operator in South Africa who was a member of the Churchill Society and he persuaded me that he was the man for the job.

In July 1999, we met up with our fellow travellers. As well as the four of us, and my aunt, Mary Soames, we had a wonderful group, several of whom I already knew. We started our tour at the Mount Nelson Hotel in Cape Town, before moving on to Durban and the battlefields of Kwa Zulu Natal where my grandfather had such thrilling adventures. We were met there by Ken Gillings who had been invaluable when I was researching my second book, *Churchill Wanted Dead or Alive*. An expert on the Boer War, but, more importantly for me, someone who had studied my grandfather's time in South Africa, he was able to introduce me to the descendants of the people who had played crucial roles in what were probably the most significant nine months of Winston's young life. If it were not for the fact that he had more than the nine lives of two cats, Winston would never have survived the several near-death experiences he suffered throughout his long life. That was quite apart from the distinct possibility of been killed on the battlefield several times, including his close encounters in South Africa.

The age of the members of our group ranged from eight to eighty. When they realised that we were taking Alexander and Sophie, then aged eleven and thirteen, two families decided to bring their own children.

From Durban, we travelled to the site of my grandfather's capture by the Boers and then on to relive the scenes portrayed in the film *Zulu* at Rorkes Drift. We stayed at Fugitives Drift the beautiful lodge belonging to David and Nicky Rattray close to the site of the battlefields of the Zulu War. David, who was tragically murdered a few years later, was an incredible storyteller, definitely in the class of Hans Christian Anderson. After an evening when we were all on the edge of our seats as he told the heroic story of Rorkes Drift, the next morning we set off for the battlefield. If anyone had told me that I would sit for three hours under the relentless African sun listening to someone telling me about the Zulu War I would have declared it impossible. Like everyone else, I was entranced and knew that I was experiencing one of the great moments of my life.

Having had our attention diverted to the Zulu War, we moved back to the Churchill theme and the Battle of Spion Kop. David Rattray showed us where Mahatma Gandhi, working as a stretcher bearer, Louis Botha, a Boer officer and the future leader of South Africa and Winston Churchill had all been close to one another during the course of the same day. Indeed, Winston wrote later about seeing wounded men being stretchered down from the battlefield when he arrived. It is highly likely that one of the bearers was Gandhi. Did their eyes meet. Neither man could have known that they would become giants of the twentieth century, but they both had a strong sense of their destiny. As we looked around at the site of one of the bloodiest battles of the Boer

War, we reflected how a stray bullet or two could have changed the history of three countries and the world beyond.

Our journey continued to Pretoria and to the Staats Model School, where my grandfather was imprisoned for four weeks and from where he made his dramatic escape. For me, the most moving part of the tour was when I stood on the spot where he had landed when he jumped over the prison wall. At that moment, when his feet touched the ground, his daring exploit place him on the international stage, where he would remain for the rest of his long life. Before that moment, people regarded him as the precocious son of a famous politician. But from then on, everyone he met began to recognise that he was destined for greatness in his own right.

The grand finale of our tour was a dinner for seventy in the Staats Model School. This led to some problems with our tour operator, who had his own agenda. He first told me that he assumed that the toasts at the dinner to the Queen, the President of South Africa and the President of the USA would be proposed by whomever in his mind were the most notable individuals amongst us. He was horrified when I told that they were all going to be proposed by children. He then told me that I should invite the minister for Tourism under the pretext that we looked a very white group and that, 'political correctness must be observed.' I assured him that it would be observed and that one of the toasts would be made by a Zulu boy, Themba, one of Alexander's and Sophie's best friends. He could not argue at that. Any other suggestions for the guest list were rebutted when I explained that the only people coming to the dinner were members of the tour, descendants of those people who had known Winston Churchill and friends of my family. Needless to say, his difficult behaviour only increased the irritation and disappointment I was feeling with the man I had chosen to be my tour guide. I have no doubt that the feeling was mutual! Despite all that, the tour was a huge success, with most of the group asking where we were going to go next. That laid the foundations for future tours *Chasing Churchill* in Morocco, cruises in the South of France, the Greek Islands, the Bosphorus, Yalta and Cuba. Because of my research trips, I was already familiar with all those places and had a network of contacts in all of them. That helped me in planning the tours and in making them enjoyable, unusual, and on the whole, trouble-free journeys in my grandfather's footsteps.

While researching in Morocco, everyone wanted to help, and every door was opened wide for me; with one exception. The Mamounia Hotel in Marrakech was the notable exception. It was the one place that had been given enormous publicity by Winston Churchill, where, apart from, the Hotel de Paris in Monte Carlo, he had spent more time than anywhere. Taking his whole office with him, he would decamp there for several weeks during the winter. He loved the warmth of its climate, its colourful atmosphere, and its stunning views for his cherished painting. I could not have written *Chasing Churchill* without the help of the airlines and hotels of the countries I visited. However, when I approached the Mamounia, I was confident that I would get a warm reception but was told that they would be happy to help me I when showed them my book contract. Annoyingly, I did not have one. I was confident of getting one but did not want to be under the pressure of a deadline and have to rush a book that had to be fitted in between speaking engagements and my children's lives.

I decided to leave Morocco to the end of the research and then wrote to the Moroccan ambassador in London expressing my surprise that their famous hotel known as 'Churchill's favourite' had given me such a frosty reception. I assured him that I would be writing about my grandfather's love for Morocco but, if I hadn't been there, I would find it difficult to describe the hotel that he liked so much. The ambassador invited me to his embassy where he assured me, I would meet several people who would give me all the help I needed. Among his guests were the head of the Moroccan Tourist Board, who would be a great support, and Annie Austin who had her own travel company and who I soon discovered was 'the Queen of Moroccan travel'.

Annie immediately went into action and arranged a wonderful two-week tour for Ken, Alexander, Sophie, and me to travel to all the places my grandfather had visited and to meet the people who had known him. We ended up at the Mamounia where we were offered one night in the Winston Churchill Suite. The children showed their appreciation for the most luxurious hotel they had ever stayed in by putting too much bubble bath into the bathtub and duly filling the bathroom with tsunami of foam. In the end, honour was saved and, in the future, when the hotel management changed, they made up for their initial clumsiness and we established a very good relationship which has continued ever since. Over the next few years, Annie arranged several enjoyable and very successful *Chasing Churchill* tours to Morocco, and she became one of my closest friends.

Not all my visits for *Chasing Churchill* were family holidays, but in conjunction with trips I had taken for other reasons earlier in my life, the list of destinations was comprehensive. It included India, Pakistan, South and East Africa, Morocco, Egypt, Cuba, the United States, Canada, Italy, Madeira, and the South of France. The only place I did not go to was the Sudan, where my grandfather fought in the last cavalry charge of the British Army at Omdurman in 1898.

I decided not to go to the Sudan, largely because there was nothing to see except sand. Also, I suspected that any descendants of Muhammad Ahmad bin Abd Allah, the Sudanese leader the British called the 'Mad Mahdi', or those of his 'Dervish' followers, may not have been too keen, given that he shot several of them, to meet Winston Churchill's granddaughter. I was wrong as recently I met the grandson of the Mahdi who is a delightful man who would certainly have added to the story.

One of the most memorable visits was to Cuba, that extraordinary place that is so full of contrasts, colour, and vibrancy. It was where my grandfather spent his 21st birthday and where, in 1895, he came under fire for the first time. After Sandhurst, in order to prove himself, he was desperate for military adventure. Unfortunately for him, the British Empire was largely at peace and there were no wars in which he could fight. However, he discovered an insurrection against Spanish rule in Cuba. So, without hesitation and with the help of his mother, he obtained permission to go from the commander-in-chief of the British Army, Lord Wolseley, who gave him an introduction to the captain general of Spain, Marshal Martinez Campos, and secured a contract from the *Daily Graphic* which paid him five guineas a piece for letters from the front.

On the day of his birthday, when a subaltern in a smart British cavalry regiment would have expected to hear the popping of champagne corks, for him there was only the popping of musketry and the whistle of a bullet that missed his head by a foot and killed the horse behind him. In his memoir, *My Early Life*, he devoted ten lines to the fate of the horse, but of his near miss, he simply commented, 'So at any rate I had been under fire. That was something. Nevertheless, I began to take a more thoughtful view of the enterprise than hitherto.' Back home, there were some who took a dim view of my grandfather's quest for adventure. The *Newcastle Leader* wrote:

> Mr Churchill was supposed to have gone to the West Indies for a holiday but spending a holiday fighting other people's battles is a rather extraordinary process, even for a Churchill.

I met many fascinating people in Cuba, but I really wanted to meet the president, the infamous communist revolutionary, Fidel Castro, who had led his country since the Cuban Revolution of 1959. After all, my grandfather was a vociferous enemy of communism and I wanted to know how Castro would react to meeting his granddaughter. Both the British embassy and my lovely guide, Yamilla, told me a meeting was highly unlikely. However, on the last morning of my visit, Yamilla could hardly contain her excitement when she told me, 'You have been invited to lunch with the Comandante!' The lunch was a huge feast, but little was eaten as the conversation flowed like a torrent. The Comandante was thinner than I had imagined, but his presence certainly filled the room. He was charming, magnetic and had twinkly eyes and a smiley sense of humour. He waved his lovely hands to great effect as he described, very proudly, how good was Cuba's education system. His very tactile manner soon had me under his spell. He asked me if I liked the beach and when I said I did, he said that he hoped I would visit him in his beach house. He gave me a bunch of exotic flowers and I gave him a bottle of my grandfather's favourite, Pol Roger champagne. He took great pleasure in telling me that he had given strict instructions that my grandfather should receive batches of his favourite Cuban cigars right up to his death. Perhaps the two famous leaders would have got on after all.

After lunch I spent the afternoon with him as he visited Elian, the little boy who had nearly drowned trying to escape to the USA. We sat shoulder to shoulder, thigh to thigh, squeezed into the back of his presidential limo. His revolver was close to hand. It suddenly occurred to me that it was common knowledge that the CIA had made hundreds of assassination attempts on his life. At that point I rather hoped the CIA might be having a day off.

Castro was a very good host. When he asked me what time my departing flight was due to leave, and I said it was imminent, he told me not to worry, as it was easy for him to order that a truck be parked in front of the plane. I was accompanied to my hotel by his assistant who reminded me that he had invited me to stay in his beach house and added, 'If you want to do something for Cuba you will accept his invitation.' I did not understand how accepting the invitation could do anything for Cuba but was certainly not going to put it to the test!

Perhaps the most memorable person I met from the point of view of nostalgia, was the man whose fishing adventures Ernest Hemingway used as the basis of his 1952 novel, *The Old Man and the Sea*. He was called, Gregorio Fuentes, and, like Santiago, the character in the novel, he was gaunt and thin, had blue eyes, came from the Canary Islands, and had a long, battle-scarred history as a fisherman. Fuentes was the captain of Hemingway's boat and the two frequently talked about the novel. Gregorio told me that he had cooked dinner for Hemingway and my grandfather when he went to Cuba in 1946, and that they had had cigar-smoking competitions. Each trying to preserve the longest amount of ash before it fell off. He was very old when I met him, but still sprightly enough, to hug me enthusiastically. Some of his memories had faded, lost in the mists of time, so he struggled to answer some of my questions. I shall never forget the tears that trickle down the deeply etched lines on his gnarled face as the memories came back to him. Gregorio died in 2002 at the age of one hundred and four.

Chasing Churchill was published in 2003. I had had enormous fun doing it; so many remarkable people, so many fascinating places and so many amazing stories. But I had run out of subjects for future books. I needed a new adventure. Following my early speaking experiences, I was reluctant to open my mouth in public unless I had to, but I soon realised that if I wanted to publicise my books, I would have to overcome my nerves.

17

TV Time

It did not take me long to identify what should be my new quest for adventure. While I was writing *Chasing Churchill*, it slowly dawned on me that I was not only a published author with a reputation of at least modest merit, I was also a sought-after speaker, acknowledged as an expert in my field. Emboldened by this, I began to think that by presenting a television series of my book, I would be able to tell my stories to audiences much bigger than the ones I could reach as an author and through my speaking engagements. I thought that if I could write well enough to be published and that people were prepared to come and listen to me speak, I felt sure I could communicate with people through the medium of television. So, rather excited by the glamour of TV, I started to ask around among friends about how to go about it. I soon got what seemed to be informed advice, that I should go and see Stewart Binns, a well-known British documentary-maker. He had won several awards, including a BAFTA, and had made quite a stir with a series of films about the Second World War using original colour film. History was obviously his thing. He seemed ideal.

At the time, Binns was working for Trans World International, a highly successful and well-known production company. TWI was part of the International Management Group, the sports and entertainment company owned by American entrepreneur, Mark McCormack. They had rather grand offices at the Hogarth Roundabout in Chiswick; their walls adorned with pictures of celebrities ranging from Kiri Te Kanawa to Martina Navratilova and from Arnold Palmer to Itzhak Perlman. As I explained to him that I wanted to make a film of *Chasing Churchill*, Binns listened politely to what I had to say. He said he thought it was a wonderful idea, a great story, and I began to think I was on my way. But there was a pause and, as always, a 'but'! He said, 'I really like it, I'm a huge Churchill fan, but what I really want to do is his whole life, the full biography.' To which I replied that it had been done several times before. 'Yes', he said, 'but we'll do it so much better. Will you help me?'

So I gulped, rather disappointed, but I realised that this man was at the top of his game, and that my best tactic would be to go along with it. It was a foot in the door. He explained what he wanted to do and what he would want from me and suggested that I could write the book of the series. He also said that if we could make a success of the big biography, we could do *Chasing Churchill* next. I did not really believe a word of it, but something was better than nothing.

Commissioned by Carlton, the series was called *Churchill*, and went out on ITV at the end of 2003. I helped with some important access to key people, including, crucially, members of the Churchill family, and I wrote the accompanying book. It was very well made and got a good reception. Ian McKellen did the narration very well and they chose John Baddeley, to reproduce my grandfather's voice, which he did very well, although in my view, no one has ever been as good as the late Robert Hardy.

It was of course, an archive-based production, but they did create some very effective reconstructions, including some things close to my heart. Because there is no colour record of my grandfather as a boy, it is often not realised that he had bright red hair. When, to play Churchill as a schoolboy, they cast a sweet young boy, Blake Woodruff, who had lovely red hair and looked just like him. This made me very happy. They also had the benefit of the letters I had used in *Love and Kisses* to reproduce some marvellous scenes at Blenheim Palace and a very poignant sequence at Harrow School when he was writing his tearful letters home to his mother.

The casting did create one amusing choice. It is true to say that few of the actors who play the adult Churchill look much like him. They have to rely heavily on the wizardry of make-up. However, Binns' team found a man called Graham Walker who was near-perfect; at least after they cut his shoulder-length hair. He was a good choice, but only in a non-speaking role. Graham was a Grumbleweed, the well-known comedy band, and from Leeds, complete with a thick Yorkshire accent; but he did bear a remarkable resemblance when in costume, complete with cigar, Homburg hat and walking stick.

The resemblance caused quite a stir when the reconstructions were done at Chartwell. The National Trust always has someone in residence in the house and one of their jobs is to supervise film crews to make sure they keep to the rules and avoid damaging anything. On the first day of filming, accompanied by the young woman from the National Trust, the crew was waiting down by the lake to shoot a scene of my grandfather walking in rueful contemplation. Graham was a little late; hair, make up and costume had to be right and Lucy Carter, the director, was a perfectionist. Eventually, Graham was ready. When he appeared, walking down from the house, he had been transformed into Winston Churchill, *circa* 1940. He was in his siren suit, with his cigar and cane and had captured the purposeful Churchillian walk perfectly. The girl from the National Trust gasped. She had been living in Chartwell with his ethereal presence for months. 'Oh my God', she blurted out, 'It's him!'

Binns was not what I imagined a BBC-trained documentary-maker to be like. He was certainly not bohemian, in fact, he wore his northern roots on his sleeve like a badge of honour. Always suited and well turned out, he was more like the Americans he worked for than the British TV stereotype. On the surface we had little in common, but got on famously and became good friends, especially when, later, he delivered on *Chasing Churchill*. He soon became 'Stewart', rather than 'Binns'.

Quite a bit of time passed, and Stewart left TWI to become Head of Production at one of its major rivals, Octagon-CSI, in Putney. Not long afterwards, he called me out of the blue and said, 'How would you like to do *Chasing Churchill*? We'll do a road trip like you do in the book, and you will be the presenter. We've got a deal with PBS in the States and a UK deal will follow for sure.' I was thrilled; it was what I had wanted to do from the moment I started researching my grandfather's travels.

Thankfully, they had the budget to do it properly. The planning process was one of the best bits. Stewart has a lovely house in the Lot in France, so the key members of the production team went down there to plan the project. It was definitely not a 'jolly'; we worked very hard. We plotted-out the whole series, worked out a schedule and did what I now know to be a shooting script. By the end, the whole series was down on paper and I began to understand how good television is made; nothing is spontaneous, it's all mapped out in precise detail.

It was a good beginning, but there were some disappointments. The first of which, was the looming presence of the production manager. They are like sergeant-majors; their job is to make the whole thing run smoothly, and strictly within budget. We also had a production assistant. They are like mini sergeant-majors, sharpening their claws for their promotion. For our film, Stewart had hired two girls who I found, to put it mildly, difficult to deal with. I am sure they felt the same about me. In retrospect I realised it would have been better to discuss our reservations, but we did not, which led to some tense moments. The first falling out was when I was told that my clothing budget for the entire series of shoots, three or four months of filming, was £300. I looked at the production assistant, who had a well-paid boyfriend in the City, and pointed out to her that on its own her jacket probably cost several times the amount of the entire clothing budget. The second shock was when I was told there was no budget for either a travelling make-up artist, or a local one for each location. I was not exactly ancient at the time, but I had turned sixty and that is old in television. To make matters worse for me, but to the delight and excitement of everyone else, the filming was going to be shot in the highly revealing detail of High Definition. Everything is done in HD now, but not then. They did send me on a one-day make-up course in Soho, but after that, I was left to my own devices, and early morning make-up and hair sessions in front of hotel mirrors.

The biggest setback was when I discovered that Stewart was not going to direct the series. I felt confident that I could do it if he was there to coax me through. He explained that he had many other projects to look after, but that his favourite editor, who would be editing the series, would be directing me and the entire shoot. However, he promised to be there to help, so, somewhat reluctantly, I accepted what was by then a *fait accompli*.

The film, a series of three one-hour programmes, began with a sequence that we shot at the 2006 passing out parade at the Royal Military Academy at Sandhurst, a ceremony that has hardly changed since my grandfather passed out in 1894. We were fortunate in being allowed to film on dress rehearsal day; the sun shone, the recruits, including Prince Harry, looked splendid in their immaculate navy-blue uniforms, gleaming swords, and mirror-polished parade boots. The series got off to a spectacular start. While we were waiting to film, I noticed that one of the cadets was loitering close by and I mentioned this to one of the crew. I then looked at him more closely and realised that it was my son, Alexander, who was in his first term at Sandhurst. I felt so guilty that I had not recognised him in his uniform and with his military haircut.

This was my first experience of filming and, with Stewart nursing me through it I gradually gained the confidence that I could do it. Our first shoot was in South Africa and the night before we left, the company gave a dinner for everyone involved in the production. This amounted to quite a number of people, not just those of us who were directly involved, but also anyone who was involved in the office. We went to a very nice restaurant and everyone was collected and taken home by chauffeur-driven cars. I was certainly impressed by the way the company looked after everyone.

It would not be long before I would discover that there was in fact quite a strict budget. We were all travelling business class to Johannesburg, but not on any subsequent journeys. Clearly someone had miscalculated the costs but, thanks to Stewart, who had insisted that as I was 'the talent', I was entitled to travel comfortably in business, while everyone else had to sit at the back of the plane. I did feel a bit awkward but not awkward enough to join them!

When we got to Heathrow, I had my first glimpse of the travelling circus that is a film shoot. It was like a house removal, with more boxes than I could count. Everything had to go through the 'Red', 'To Declare' Channel to do all the paperwork and what is called a 'carnet' to import and export expensive equipment. Not only that, it had to happen at both ends of the journey.

South Africa, where my grandfather had had his Boer War adventures, went very well. I was anxious at first; after all, a huge investment had been made in the film and several broadcasters were expecting a highly polished product and I had to deliver. I could speak in public and I knew what to say but speaking directly into the camera is difficult to do, particularly when you have to engage an audience you cannot see. But I soon got the hang of it and all the stuff about, 'walking and talking' and the various nuances of how to turn to the camera and how to turn away from it. It soon became exciting rather than nerve-wracking, but there were more anxieties to come. I was on familiar territory in South Africa and the filming followed itineraries I had travelled many times before. I knew most of the people we met, especially the wonderful Ken Gillings, who was our guide. Ken had managed to find even more Churchillian people and places than he had found for me some years before. One was the pub in Estcourt, KwaZulu-Natal, where my grandfather had held court in 1899, and, famously, told the local stationmaster, 'Mark my words, one day, I will be prime minister of England.' We interviewed Derek Clegg, the station-master's grandson, in the very same pub where he recalled his uncle telling him that almost four decades later, in May 1940, he had picked up the newspaper and exclaimed, 'My God, he's done it!'

Just as South Africa has changed, so has the pub. In my grandfather's day, Estcourt was a White and Asian town, with the black community living on the outskirts, in what would later become townships. The local African population would not have been able to drink in the pub, although they may have been in the back, washing beer pots. But, post-Apartheid, Estcourt is now a predominantly Black town. In 1899, the pub, on a busy street corner right in the heart of the town, would have resembled a Victorian pub in England, but is now much more like a shebeen, complete with one or two characters we all felt we should keep a close eye on. Thankfully, Ken was with us, who spoke fluent Zulu, and everything went well. The locals remained very friendly, especially after we bought several rounds of drinks.

There was another particularly emotive location, which I remember vividly. Ken's knowledge of the ground and military affairs meant that he was able to describe in great detail what had happened there. It was a chilling experience to re-live the event, standing on the very spot where it happened. My grandfather, always wanting to be in the thick of it, was on an armoured train, loaded with British soldiers, which was performing a scouting expedition between Frere and Chieveley in what was then called the British Natal Colony.

It was November 1899. A Boer Kommando force had sabotaged the track and the steam train crashed into it, de-railing several of the carriages. The Boers then opened fire from their high ground. As shells roared around him and bullets ricocheted off the sides of the train, the war correspondent immediately transformed himself into a military commander and took control. Acting like a veteran, he braved the intimidating fire for more than an hour as he organised the soldiers to free the train. He was able to get several of the men to safety, but then attempted to save more. As he did so, he was confronted by a Boer officer on horseback. The officer raised his Mauser rifle from about forty yards.

Churchill went for his revolver in its holster, but it was not there. He had left it with the engine driver for protection. He had no choice, but to surrender. The empty holster was a blessing. Had he fired on the Boer, his revolver would have been no match for a Mauser in the hands of an experienced marksman. My grandfather would have become a tiny footnote in the history of the Boer War and of no future consequence in the history of his nation. But high stakes were what drove him on. 'There is no ambition I cherish so keenly as to gain a reputation for personal courage', he had confided to his younger brother, Jack, two years earlier.

There is further irony in the fact that the Boer officer who captured him was none other than Louis Botha, later the first prime minister of Transvaal, and someone who was to become a great friend. In *My Early Life*, Churchill described him:

> Few men that I have known have interested me more than Louis Botha. An acquaintance formed in strange circumstances and upon an almost unbelievable introduction ripened into a friendship which I greatly valued. I saw in this grand, rugged figure, the Father of his country, the wise and profound statesman, the farmer-warrior, the crafty hunter of the wilderness, the deep, sure man of solitude.

Churchill was imprisoned in the Staat's Model School in Pretoria, which had been converted to a prison. Although the Boers treated POWs well and he was allowed to purchase newspapers, cigarettes, and beer, he despised his imprisonment, 'more than I have ever hated any other period in my whole life.' What frustrated him most was the possibility that he was missing out on further opportunities for glory. 'I had cut myself out of the whole of this exciting war with all its boundless possibilities of adventure and advancement,' he bemoaned.

However, on the night of 12 December 1899, he hid in the prison latrine before scaling a ten-foot high wall and made a break for freedom. He had no map, no ability to speak the Boer language and just, 'four slabs of melting chocolate and a crumbling biscuit' in his pocket. But he was armed with his extraordinary self-belief. He was sure he could navigate the 300-mile journey through enemy territory to neutral Portuguese East Africa, especially when guarded by what he was sure was his destiny, which had, after all, determined that he was ordained for greatness.

The Boers launched a massive manhunt. Posters were printed offering a £25 reward for his capture, 'Dead or Alive'. Britain became captivated by Churchill's saga. His public life had begun. So I got a shiver as I stood on the exact spot at the bottom of the prison wall in Pretoria where my grandfather's feet had landed when making his escape. From that moment, his fame was assured, and he would be in the spotlight of world affairs for the rest of his very long life.

Through the evening crowds in Pretoria, he made his way to the railway station and stowed away on a coal train heading east towards East Africa. The following evening, the train stopped at Clewer siding near Witbank on the Highveld. He saw a light in a house in the distance and decided to knock on the door. Fortune favours the brave, especially if you are Winston Churchill. The door he chose to knock on was that of John Howard, the only Englishman in the area, and manager of the Transvaal and Delagoa Bay Colliery. Churchill was fed well and later hidden in the underground stables of the mine. With only rats for company, he spent six days underground, before Howard organised his onward journey to freedom. He was hidden in a railway wagon loaded with wool and bound for Mozambique. The train finally reached its destination, Lourenço Marques, on 21 December. When he crossed the border, he reached for a revolver provided by Howard, waved it in the air and shouted, 'I'm Winston Churchill and I'm bloody well free!'

Greeted by an extremely dishevelled young man, the British consul was not immediately convinced of Churchill's identity, but, two days later, a cable reached Howard at Witbank. It read, 'Goods arrived safely'.

The production team pulled off a significant coup about the escape. They managed to find some steam enthusiasts and a small station, which still had the look of railways of old, complete with wooden wagons, which bore an uncanny resemblance to the ones in which my grandfather escaped. It made for a wonderful sequence and fond memories for me.

Although Churchill had finally achieved the glory he had always sought, he opted to continue covering the war, and fighting in it as well. He participated in the Battle of Spion Kop where a bullet severed a feather on his hat. When Pretoria fell in June 1900, Churchill rode into the city on horseback and led the liberation of the 180 soldiers remaining in the prison where he had once been confined. When he returned to England, in a lovely gesture, my grandfather commissioned eight inscribed gold watches to be sent to those who had helped him escape. Six of them have survived and I have been fortunate enough to have handled three of them. A century later, the watches have become prized possessions and, sadly, in one family, the cause of a feud.

As the South Africa shoot progressed, we all got on quite well; it was a success. But, after a while, the gloss of filming wears off and tedium sets in. The countless 'takes', trying to repeat what was said in the last one, the standing around while the camera is reset, and the long hours and long days, become exhausting. Not only that, there was a bombshell towards the end. Stewart suddenly announced that he had to return to London. There was something back in the office, a crisis, the nature of which I never discovered, and he had to go. I was left isolated. Ominously, there had been warning signs that suggested that the director and I might have a few issues. He was very young and had never directed before. He was nervous and the more uncomfortable he became, the more his complexion deteriorated, and his demeanour worsened. That, of course, made it doubly difficult for me to perform in front of the camera. So I was left with a director with whom I did not get along, and two young women who seemed to be watching me like hawks to ensure that I kept to the straight and narrow. Thankfully, I had struck up a friendship with the director of photography and the sound recordist, who became my saviours and got me through the series. Unfortunately, we were not able to socialise much, as, in the evenings, they had to go through what had been shot during the day and get everything ready for the next morning.

As filming for the series continued, the atmosphere in the team worsened. The director knew what he wanted in terms of the logic of filming and how to put it on screen, but his people skills were virtually non-existent. This led to more and more tension between him and me and within the team. Looking back, I should have dug my heels in about several things, but I was so determined to make a success of it, I simply gritted my teeth and got on with it.

The locations were the best part of it all. I spent my birthday on a camel by the pyramids in Egypt, where we re-created the famous race between my grandfather and T. E. Lawrence, Lawrence of Arabia. We rode horses in Cuba. We went to Morocco, where we captured a famous moment enjoyed by my grandfather and US President Franklin Roosevelt. It took place in January 1943, at the end of the Casablanca Conference, just a few months before I was born. Casablanca was the meeting that produced the 'Casablanca Declaration', demanding the 'unconditional surrender' of Germany and the Axis Powers, and decided on the invasion of Sicily rather than an attack in northern Europe.

After the conference, and in the midst of the greatest crisis of modern times, my grandfather said to Roosevelt, 'You cannot come all this way to North Africa without seeing Marrakech. Let us spend two days there. I must be with you when you see the sun go down on the Atlas Mountains.' My grandfather loved Marrakech. He called it, 'The most lovely spot in the whole world.'

So, with an armoured car escort on the ground and fighter aircraft in the air, the two leaders made the five-hour journey across the desert to Marrakech, the ancient city my grandfather christened, 'the Paris of the South'. They had a picnic in the desert, the menu for which is not recorded, but, knowing my grandfather, I suspect it was a little more elaborate than a few sandwiches and a glass of cold beer. When they arrived in Marrakech, they stayed at the Villa Taylor, a handsome house owned by an American family, but leased to the American consul, Kenneth Pendar. My Grandfather insisted that Roosevelt accompany him up the Villa's tower so that they could experience the spectacular sunset together. Although not well-known at the time, the President, who had contracted polio at the age of thirty-nine, was wheelchair-bound and had to be carried up to the tower by two burly marines.

Reclining on a divan, Roosevelt, overwhelmed by the view, said, 'I feel like a sultan; you may kiss my hand, my dear!' My grandfather's doctor, Lord Moran, witnessed the scene:

> The President was carried up the winding stairs to the roof-top, his paralysed legs dangling like the limbs of a ventriloquist's dummy, limp and flaccid. We stood gazing at the purple hills where the light was changing every second.

Roosevelt left Marrakech the next morning. At lunchtime, my grandfather, who had accompanied the President to the airport in his dragon embroidered dressing gown, returned to the villa and got out his paints to capture the view the two men had enjoyed. It would be the only painting he would commit to canvas during the entire war.

Sadly, Villa Taylor is now empty and run-down. It is said that the owner, a staunch Republican, was so incensed that a Democrat had slept in her bed, that soon after the visit she sold the house. In spite of her disgust at what had taken place when she heard about the painting, she offered to buy it, but my grandfather told her that he had already made a gift of it to the very man whose nocturnal presence had so upset her. The painting was subsequently sold to Brad Pitt and Angelina Jolie for over two million dollars and, as mentioned earlier, was sold after their divorce by Angelina Jolie for over eleven million dollars in 2021— at least they did not cut it in half!

Fortunately for the film, I was able to persuade some friends of mine in Marrakech to let us recreate the scene from their tower, which was a close replica of Villa Taylor. It was one of the highlights of the film and particularly memorable for me as, like my grandfather, I have a great affection for Morocco. As he flew to Cairo, refreshed after the delights of Marrakech, he could take great comfort from the turning tide of the war. The Soviet Red Army was close to forcing the surrender of Germany's 6th Army in the Battle of Stalingrad, the invasion of Sicily had been agreed and plans for the invasion of Europe in 1944 were in progress.

From Cairo, he wrote to the Dominion prime ministers on 27 January 1943:

> I cannot help feeling that things are quite definitely better than when I was last in Cairo, when the enemy was less than seventy miles away. If we should succeed in retaining the initiative in all theatres, as does not seem impossible ... we might well regard the world situation as by no means devoid of favourable features.

Although modest in terms of Churchillian rhetoric, there was no doubt that he left Morocco in a buoyant mood.

Shoots followed in New York, Washington and California and we re-created some special moments in the South of France and on Onassis's legendary yacht, the *Christina*. In California we went to Hearst Castle at San Simeon, where he had stayed, and to Hollywood, where he struck up his friendship with Charlie Chaplin. Our guide, a rather outlandish man, tried to get me to walk like Chaplin. The director was tempted of course, but I drew the line at silly walks.

In the South of France, we focused on my grandfather's love of painting and tried to capture the solace it gave him. For him, to escape to 'batheable and paintable' places was a very important contrast to his incredibly busy and stressful life. While in France, we interviewed Anthony Montague Browne, my grandfather's private secretary and close family friend. Anthony told me several stories for the camera, one of which was very amusing, the other, very moving.

The funny story involved Frank Sinatra. After being in the casino in Monte Carlo, Grandpapa was waiting for his car, when Sinatra and his posse of people came past. Upon seeing who it was, Sinatra rushed forwards and grabbed my grandfather's hand and shook it vigorously, saying, 'I've been wanting to do that for years', and marched off. My grandfather turned to Anthony and said, 'Who the hell was that?'

The other story, a very emotive one, I shared with Anthony. It was June 1962, and we were staying at the Hotel de Paris in Monte Carlo when my grandfather fell in his room and broke his hip. It was very serious. So much so that he made Anthony promise that he would die in England. As I explained earlier, I flew back with him, fearing the worst, but, after two months in hospital, he survived, but was never quite the same again.

Anthony, tears rolling down his cheeks, described his feelings at the time. 'Although he had spurts of humour. He liked to be reminded of things. It went away and then it came back. And the rest is silence.'

The United States produced some wonderful anecdotes. We interviewed Rudi Giuliani, the former mayor of New York, who is a very engaging character and went to the house in Brooklyn where Jennie Jerome, my grandfather's mother, was born. The visit produced one of those oddities of history. When my grandfather made a very public pilgrimage to discover his mother's birthplace in 1953, complete with crowds of sightseers and photographers, he was taken to 426 Henry Street in the Cobble Hill District where he unveiled a plaque. Apparently when the Brooklyn dignitaries heard of the impending Churchill visit, they thought that the real birthplace, at nearby 197 Amity Street, was too modest. So, somewhat strangely, he was shown Henry Street instead. Fortunately, we were able to sort fact from fiction and filmed at the correct house.

After Brooklyn, we went to Virginia to interview Senator Harry Byrd Jr, the former senator for Virginia and the delightful son of Harry Byrd, the governor of Virginia in the 1920s. I had met him when I was researching *Chasing Churchill* and he gave me the oldest living memory from the youngest witness. He vividly remembered meeting my grandfather at the tender age of eleven during his 1929 grand tour of North America. He stayed with the Byrds at the governor's mansion in Richmond so that he could visit the battlefields of the Civil War. When they first met, my grandfather assumed young Harry was a junior member of the mansion's staff and asked him to run and get him a newspaper. When he returned with the newspaper under his arm, he was given a tip of a quarter, a coin he kept for the rest of his life. Winston stayed for ten days, quite long enough to test the patience of any host. When he returned from the battlefields each evening, he made himself very much at home; rather too much at home for the lady of the house, The governor's wife, Anne. One night, my grandfather kept all the guests waiting to enjoy their virginia ham while a member of staff ran to the local store to buy his favourite mustard. But that was only a minor incident. Apart from needing mustard with his ham, he liked to live by what he called 'tummy time', so he wanted to decide when the meals would be served. Not only that, he also wanted to determine what the menus should be. On one occasion, during a state banquet in his honour, the waiter came up to him with a tray of chicken and asked him which part of the bird he would like, to which he replied, 'The breast, please.' Clearly dismayed, the woman next to him said, 'Mr Churchill, in America we say, "white meat or dark meat."' The next morning, the lady in question received a little posy of flowers from my grandfather with a note saying, 'Please attach these to your white meat.'

His other idiosyncrasies, beyond those of the dining table, like walking around the mansion in his underwear, did not meet with the approval of the first lady of Virginia either! When my grandfather finally left and the governor and his wife waved him goodbye, their son remembers his mother turning to her husband and saying, 'Don't you ever invite that dreadful man here again!'

From Washington, we drove to nearby Alexandria, just across the Potomac River. Located in the beautiful old town district of the city, Christchurch parish church was built in 1773 by Colonel James Wren, a descendant of Sir Christopher Wren. You can see the influence in the lovely symmetry of the building. The interior is a treasure, with a gorgeous wine glass pulpit.

George Washington and Robert E. Lee were both parishioners of Christchurch. Until the twenty-first century, it was a tradition that sitting presidents attend a service there. On 1 January 1942, to celebrate World Day of Prayer for Peace, my grandfather and President Roosevelt visited the church. They sat together with my grandfather sitting proudly in Washington's pew. It was an evocative gathering as it was just three weeks after the Japanese attack on Pearl Harbor, which plunged the world into a global conflict even more catastrophic than the war in Europe.

In one of the most emotional interviews in *Chasing Churchill*, Marguerite Lamond a parishioner of Christchurch, who, as a young woman, was one of the few people still alive who was there that day. She described the ceremony for me and remembered the tears pouring down my grandfather's face as they sang, 'The Battle Hymn of the Republic'. With tears welling in her own eyes, she said:

Seeing the two men united in prayer and singing together was very moving. It is a memory that will live with me forever. We left the church knowing that there would be peace in our time.

The final scene of *Chasing Churchill*, the memory of which I still find very moving, was filmed on the *Havengore* on the Thames, when I retraced my grandfather's final journey from Tower Pier to Waterloo during his state funeral. This time there were no crowds, no dockyard cranes being lowered in homage, but it was very poignant all the same. By the end, I had no idea what the film would be like. I had my doubts because the atmosphere during the filming had been so tense. However, the director came into his own in the edit. With Stewart at his side and with beautiful music by the composer, Chris Elliott, it was a treat to watch. Everyone loved it and it got an excellent response, particularly in the United States, where it seemed to be on PBS constantly. Even to this day, I get calls from America to say that they have just seen it. It never made any money and I made almost nothing from it apart from a small fee, but it gave my speaking career a big boost. The series was shown on Discovery here in the UK, which gave even more impetus to my speaking engagements and requests for media interviews.

18

Never Give In

The only problem with the success of *Chasing Churchill* was that I had got the taste for television and wanted to do more. I love telling stories. Years ago, I was terrified of opening my mouth in public but now I get a thrill every time I stand up to make a speech. Presenting television is equally exciting especially as the audience is so much bigger. To that end, Stewart and I have several projects in the pipeline. One of them, *In My Grandmother's Footsteps*, will tell the story of my grandmother, Clementine's relationship with the Soviet Red Cross during the war and her amazing visit around a war-devastated Soviet Union in 1945. Sadly, her visit coincided with the sudden end of the war, so she was not in London to share my grandfather's moment of glory on the balcony of Buckingham Palace on VE Day.

From time to time, we have come close to getting the series away, including some promotional filming in the Kremlin, which was fascinating. But each time we made progress, diplomatic relations between the Kremlin and the West seemed to take a turn for the worst and the plans came to nothing.

Through one of their local broadcasters, WNET in New York, we also got very close to a new deal with PBS for something that would have been exciting to do. It was called *Matriarchs and Mistresses*, a series about six remarkable women, all associated with the Spencer-Churchill dynasty: Sarah Churchill, née Jennings, duchess of Marlborough; Georgiana Cavendish, née Spencer, duchess of Devonshire; Jennie Jerome, Lady Randolph Churchill; Clementine Churchill; Pamela Churchill Harriman; and Diana Spencer, princess of Wales.

Another pet project, which, amazingly, has not been done, is *Churchill and America*, a series about my grandfather's lifelong relationship with his 'other country', the United States, the land of his mother's birth. It would have been very timely in 2020, the eightieth anniversary of him becoming prime minister, but COVID-19 put paid to that idea.

Over the years since *Chasing Churchill*, my speaking career has blossomed. I do tours here in the UK and lecture tours in America and I have developed an outstanding relationship with Tauck Tours, the up-market American travel company, which now organises travel experiences all over the world. In fact, at the beginning of the relationship, I was involved in a bidding war with one of Tauck's rivals. Fortunately, Tauck won the war and we have been friends ever since. Before Tauck, I had done some speaking engagements on transatlantic crossings on several occasions on the *Queen Elizabeth 2*, and cruise ships.

On 29 October 1941, in the midst of one of the most difficult periods during the war, my grandfather visited his old school, Harrow, to attend 'Harrow Songs'. 'Songs' is a famous Harrow tradition dating back to 1864. He had attended Songs ten months earlier, after many years of indifference towards the school, where he had not been happy. His change of heart came about when he heard that two high explosive bombs had hit Harrow's grounds and that the school had decided to stay on Harrow Hill rather than be evacuated to the countryside. Perhaps he needed the famous songs and the bright young faces of the boys to find inspiration to continue the perilous fight. The whole of Europe was either neutral or under Nazi rule. The situation in North Africa was dire, with Tobruk under siege by Rommel's Afrika Corps. After five months of Operation Barbarossa, the German army was at the gates of Moscow and the Siege of Leningrad had begun. Joseph Stalin had recalled Marshal Zhukov to defend Moscow and ordered the eastwards evacuation of the Soviet government and much of the country's manufacturing. In the wake of the German advance into the Soviet Union, Nazi death squads were committing atrocities on an unprecedented scale. All opposition was annihilated, and Jews were being slaughtered in their hundreds of thousands. To make matters even worse, Hideki Tojo had just been made prime minister of Japan, clearing the way for the attack on Pearl Harbor just a few weeks later. There were many dark days during the war, and this was certainly one of them. In fact, in his address to the boys, he referred to 'dark days':

Do not let us speak of darker days: let us speak rather of sterner days. These are not dark days; these are great days—the greatest days our country has ever lived; and we must all thank God that we have been allowed, each of us according to our stations, to play a part in making these days memorable in the history of our race.

In an earlier part of his address, he produced one of his most famous speeches:

I am addressing myself to the School—surely from this period of ten months, this is the lesson: never give in, never give in, never, never, never, never—in nothing, great or small, large or petty—never give in, except to convictions of honour and good sense...

Although I do not wish to claim any feats or virtues even remotely akin to my grandfather's achievements, his 'never give in' words remain inspirational for me. I did not have to fight fascism, Hitler's panzers, the opprobrium of the Dardanelles, or years in the political wilderness, but I did have to fight social conventions, parental expectations, and my personal inhibitions. No matter how challenging, I never gave in to any of those. I do not indulge in introspection, but there is no doubt that throughout my life, I have had to go against the grain. Most of all, I have had to resist what was expected of me and the temptations of 'marrying well', with its many comforts and privileges. Although I was the granddaughter of Winston Churchill and the daughter of a government minister, I was a woman. In the twenty-first century, it may well be that it would be expected of me to follow in the footsteps of a famous parent or grandparent, but in the late fifties, early sixties, a woman from my background was expected to become the anchor in the life of a great, titled or wealthy man, but not expected to aspire to those things herself.

Advancing age is disturbing for all of us. Infirmity, mental or physical, is a terror we all fear and sooner or later have to face. On the other hand, every year brings new experiences, wisdom, and memories to savour. I enjoy my many memories. I can remember rationing and the lamp-lighter who lit the gas lamp outside my bedroom window every night and put them out again in the morning. My favourite childhood poem was Robert Louis Stevenson's, *Leerie the Lamplighter*:

> My tea is nearly ready and the sun has left the sky;
> It's time to take the window to see Leerie going by;
> For every night at teatime and before you take your seat,
> With lantern and with ladder he comes posting up the street.
> Now Tom would be a driver and Maria go to sea,
> And my papa's a banker and as rich as he can be;
> But I, when I am stronger and can choose what I'm to do,
> Oh Leerie, I'll go round at night and light the lamps with you!
>
> For we are very lucky, with a lamp before the door,
> And Leerie stops to light it as he lights so many more;
> And O! before you hurry by with ladder and with light,
> O Leerie, see a little child and nod to him tonight!

Stevenson painted very vivid images with his writing, saying that electric light was, 'that ugly blinding glare' and 'a lamp for a nightmare.' I suppose he was a romantic, especially about the past, and I think I am the same.

I remember the extraordinary freedom of my childhood, a childhood denied to most children today. Even though, by modern standards, there was a drabness about post-war London and its countless bombsites, for me, the streets were my playground. As young as six or seven my mother would send me to Frank Wand's sweet shop to buy her some chocolate. The countryside was an adventure park. Now, there are so many dangers, real or imagined, that inhibit the freedom of childhood. I have happy memories wherever I go in London and although I loved the twenty years that Ken and I spent in Devon and Wiltshire, I am happy to be back.

I have lived through an era of extraordinary change, both in my life and in the world in general, and it is surely enough for any of us to have been fortunate to have lived a full life. It would be foolish not to embrace change. 'Modern conveniences' have changed our lives, largely for the better. Domestic appliances and, later, mobile phones and computers are part of a technological revolution that is changing the world and creating new excitements and challenges. But more recent innovations, particularly what is known as 'social media', might also be dubbed, 'anti-social media', and I find them more of bind than a boon.

Apart from the obvious threats to the simplicity of our lives from the darker fringes of social media, I regret that letter-writing is a dying convention. It is sad to think that future historians will not be able to enjoy, as I did, the tangible thrill of unearthing a treasure trove of childish, sometimes tear-stained, letters.

As is often the case with the children or grandchildren of famous people, I am often asked if my grandfather cast an oppressive shadow across my life or illuminated it with a warm glow. Indeed, I am aware that many people's lives have been blighted by their familial inheritance. For example, someone once told me that the son of the great Australian cricketer, Sir Donald Bradman, changed his name from Bradman to Bradsen to distance himself from his famous father.

In my case, the presence of Winston Churchill in my life, has been a source of adventure, excitement, and pride. His presence has enriched my life and set the route for my personal journey in ways that fill me with joy and wonder whenever I think about them. As a result of my particular accident of birth, I have been given many opportunities and privileges. My grandfather's particular legacy has taken me all over the world to many amazing places and given me the chance to meet so many extraordinary people. They were not just the great and the good, but also quite ordinary people, who often turn out to be more fascinating to meet and talk with than their more illustrious peers.

I have also enjoyed another delight; in that, even though he has been dead for well over fifty years, he has not faded in my memory; quite the reverse. When I knew him well, he was already old and rapidly became much older and very frail. However, because I have since spent decades discovering the details of his life, especially his young life and I am constantly being asked questions about him. I have read countless new books about his life and have seen him portrayed in a conveyor belt of films. So, rather than fading in my memory, he is constantly coming into sharper and sharper focus.

Inevitably when I knew him, he was but a shadow of his former self. Now, every day provides new and better insights, and I am able to enjoy the man as he was when he was in his prime, all guns blazing. He was a man to be admired and feared, loathed, and adored. He could be extremely demanding, only the strongest of those who worked with him prevailed and he certainly did not suffer fools. However, when one considers that the words, 'greatness', 'heroic', 'legendary' and many other accolades are readily associated with his name, I am so happy that I was lucky enough to know and love him.

I am now much closer to the end of my life than I am to its beginning. Like all of us of a certain age, who have seen extraordinary change in their lifetime, I do think about the future, especially as change seems to be happening ever more quickly. I fear for my children and grandchildren and what the legacy of my generation and generations past might be for the welfare of the world we live in. I suppose we must hope that our immediate descendants have the good sense to take the measures that are needed to preserve our species and all the other creatures that share our world.

I wonder what my grandfather would make of it if he was around now and in his prime. Would he turn his warrior instincts to fighting for the climate and the natural world and against those who seem hell-bent on undermining the delicate balance of our planet? I have no doubt he would rail against terrorism and the world's many malign forces. But, given that he was an avid student of history and therefore an accurate predictor of the future, I wonder if he would have seen his destiny as saving us from ourselves?

Apart from my many adventures and my professional guise, by far the most important thing in my life has been my family. I have four children and three grandchildren. I have been incredibly lucky. My children are all very kind to me and I am extremely proud of all the many different things they have done. In that sense, I feel completely fulfilled.

I have had three husbands and managed, more or less, to stay on extremely good terms with all of them. Michael brought me Africa and gave me my son, Justin; Dennis brought me Italy and gave me Dominic;

and Ken brought me my career as a storyteller and gave me Alexander and Sophie. As well as being lucky in life, I have also been lucky in love.

I do not have many regrets, but one is that I did not hang on so well to some of my old friends. I still have a lovely circle, but the gaps appeared when I married Ken, and, progressively, we moved further and further away from London. That made face-to-face contact very difficult. Then we had children when most of my friends were having grandchildren. Not only that, as the school ties increased, it became more and more difficult to see old friends. Local friendships were equally problematic. Apart from the fact that Ken and I were a generation older than most of the other parents, school was a six-day a week commitment and Sundays became very precious for the four of us to spend together.

Now, as a single woman, living happily with Daisy, my cavapoo, in London, some of my closest friends are scattered far and wide in South Africa, Italy, Hong Kong, and America. Some are living in retirement in the country but happily they come to London. So, here is my life, seventy-eight years and counting. I hope it has been worth committing to paper and that it is seen to be moderately interesting. When several people persuaded me to write an account of my life and times, I doubted that anyone would find it of any interest. If you are still reading, I am relieved and grateful.

My grandfather wrote:

When I survey the scene of my past life, I have no doubt that I do not wish to live it over again. Not even the opportunity of making a different set of mistakes and experiencing a different set of adventures and successes would lure me. The journey has been enjoyable and well worth making ... once.

For my part, I intend to follow his instruction to those around him and will 'KBO' (keep buggering on)!